Toad of Toad Hall

Toad of Toad Hall

*

A PLAY FROM
KENNETH GRAHAME'S BOOK
The Wind in the Willows

BY

A. A. MILNE

A Magnet Book

Hardback edition first published
11 April 1929
by Methuen & Co Ltd
Reprinted thirty times
Reprinted 1970 by Methuen Children's Books Ltd,
11 New Fetter Lane, London EC 4P 4EE
Reprinted four times
Reprinted 1981
ISBN 0 416 38770 5

Paperback edition first published 1970
by Methuen Children's Books Ltd
Reprinted ten times
Reprinted 1984
ISBN 0 416 07790 0

Applications regarding Amateur Performances
of this play should be addressed to Messrs Samuel
French Ltd, 26 Southampton Street, London
WC 2. Applications for other rights to Messrs
Curtis Brown Ltd, 1 Craven Hill, London
W 2 3EW

Printed and bound in Great Britain by
Hazell Watson & Viney Limited,
Member of the BPCC Group,
Aylesbury, Bucks

Introduction

*

THERE are familiarities which we will allow only ourselves to take. Your hands and my hands are no cleaner
than anybody else's hands, yet the sort of well-thumbed
bread-and-butter which we prefer is that on which we
have placed our own thumbs. It may be that to turn Mr
Kenneth Grahame into a play is to leave unattractive
fingermarks all over him, but I love his books so much
that I cannot bear to think of anybody else disfiguring
them. That is why I accepted a suggestion, which I should
have refused in the case of any other book as too difficult
for me, that I should dramatize *The Wind in the Willows*.

There are two well-known ways in which to make a
play out of a book. You may insist on being faithful to the
author, which means that the scene in the aeroplane on
page 673 must be got in somehow, however impossible
dramatically, or, with somebody else's idea in your
pocket, you may insist on being faithful to yourself,
which means that by the middle of Act III everybody will
realize how right the original author was to have made a
book of it. There may be a third way, in which case I
have tried to follow it. If, as is more likely, there isn't,
then I have *not* made a play of *The Wind in the Willows*.
But I have, I hope, made some sort of entertainment, with
enough of Kenneth Grahame in it to appease his many
admirers, and enough of me in it to justify my name
upon the title-page.

Of course I have left out all the best parts of the book;

and for that, if he has any knowledge of the theatre, Mr Grahame will thank me. With a Rat and Mole from the Green Room Club, a Baby Otter from Conti, a Pan from Clarkson's, and a wind (off) whispering in the reeds of Harker, we are not going to add any fresh thrill to the thrill which the loveliness of *The Piper at the Gates of Dawn* has already given its readers. Whether there is, indeed, any way of putting these animals on the stage must be left to managers, professional and amateur, to find out. But it seemed clear to me that Rat and Toad, Mole and Badger could only face the footlights with hope of success if they were content to amuse their audiences. There are both beauty and comedy in the book, but the beauty must be left to blossom there, for I, anyhow, shall not attempt to transplant it.

But can one transplant even the comedy? Perhaps it has happened to you, as it has certainly happened to me, that you have tried to explain a fantastic idea to an entirely matter-of-fact person. 'But they *don't*,' he says, and 'You *can't*,' and 'I don't see *why*, just because—' and 'Even if you assume that—' and 'I thought you said just now that he *hadn't*.' By this time you have thrown the ink-pot at him, with enough of accuracy, let us hope, to save you from his ultimatum, which is this: 'However fantastic your assumption, you *must* work it out logically' – that is to say, realistically.

To such a mind *The Wind in the Willows* makes no appeal, for it is not worked out logically. In reading the book, it is necessary to think of Mole, for instance, sometimes as an actual mole, sometimes as such a mole in human clothes, sometimes as a mole grown to human size, sometimes as walking on two legs, sometimes on four. He is a mole, he isn't a mole. What is he? I don't *him*. You see, he lives underground a good deal, and doesn't go out into society much, so I should think he'd be rather simple, and not liking to talk about himself, and just saying 'Yes' and 'No', and waiting to be asked before he has a second cup. And then Mr Badger – of course he's grey, and much older than the others, and very fatherly – and sleeps a good deal with a handkerchief over his face, and says 'Now, now, now' and 'Well, well, well' when he's woken up. And Mr Otter—

NURSE Well, well, well, fancy that now! Why, you might almost have seen them at it, the way you talk.

MARIGOLD I have.

NURSE Never!

MARIGOLD Yes. One morning. I came out here early, oh, ever so early. Nobody was up – you weren't up, and the birds weren't up, and even the sun wasn't up – and everything was so still that there was no sound in all the world, except just the wind in the willows, whispering ever so gently.

NURSE (*professionally*) What your poor mother would have said— (*Eagerly*) Well, and what happened?

MARIGOLD I don't know. I sat there and waited for everything to wake up, and then by and by I heard something – music, very thin and clear and far off – and then – well, then there was the sun, and it was daylight, and it seemed as if I had just woken up myself. But it was all different. Something had happened. I didn't know what, but I seemed to understand more than I did before – to have been *with* them.

NURSE Mr Toad and Mr Mole and all them?

MARIGOLD Yes. I've never really seen them since. I pretend to talk to them, just as if they were really there,

but— (*With sudden excitement*) Wouldn't it be lovely
if they suddenly came out and began to talk – Mole
from under the ground there, and the Water Rat from
his hole in the bank, and the old Badger from the dead
leaves in the ditch, and Mr Toad—

NURSE   I should be that frightened, if they were all big.

MARIGOLD   Oh no, you wouldn't, because they
wouldn't know *we* were here. We should just listen to
them, without their knowing anything about it. (*She
calls out*) Mr Mole! Mr Rat! Mr Toad! Oh, Nurse,
wouldn't it be *lovely*?

NURSE   Oo, I can hear something! Listen!

MARIGOLD   That's the music again. Quick! Hide!

*It is dark suddenly, and we hear music, very thin and clear
and far off: 'the horns of Elfland faintly blowing'. Gradu-
ally it grows light again. There is no* NURSE, *no* MARI-
GOLD *now. But near where* MARIGOLD *was lying there
is a curious upheaval going on. The earth moves and humps
up and falls back again. Somebody is at work underneath.
We hear breathings and mutterings. In a little while we
can distinguish words. It is our old friend* MOLE.

MOLE (*as he comes laboriously into the daylight*)   Scrape
and scratch and scrabble and scrooge – scrooge and
scrabble and scrape and scratch – up we go, up we go!
. . . Pop! (*He stands up and brushes himself.*) Ah! (*He
takes a deep breath of daylight.*) This is fine! This is better
than whitewash. Hang spring-cleaning! (*He walks about,
making ecstatic noises to himself.*) Oh, what a day! Oh
my, oh my, oh my! Blow spring-cleaning! (*He rubs his
eyes with his paw.*) Is that a River? Oh my, oh my! *Bother*
spring-cleaning!

The river has hollowed out a little bay here, so that NURSE
and MARIGOLD, *from where they are sitting in Box B,*

can see their own side of the bank, where it bends round in a curve, and they can see RAT'S *front door and they can see bright eyes and a sharp friendly face, with whiskers, as the* WATER RAT *comes out of it.*

RAT Hallo, Mole!

MOLE Hallo, Rat!

RAT Don't seem to have seen you about before.

MOLE (*shyly*) I – I don't go out much, as a rule.

RAT (*cheerily*) Prefer home-life? *I* know. Very good thing too in its way.

MOLE Yes, you see, I— This is a river, isn't it?

RAT *The* River.

MOLE (*simply*) I've never seen a river before.

RAT (*staggered*) Never seen a— You never— Well, I— What *have* you been doing then?

MOLE Is it as nice as that?

RAT Nice? My dear young friend, believe me, it's the *only* thing. There is *nothing* – absolutely nothing – half so much worth doing as simply messing about by a river. (*Dreamily*) Simply messing – messing about by a river – or *in* a river – or *on* a river. It doesn't matter which.

MOLE But what do you *do*?

RAT Nothing. Just mess about. That's the charm of it; you're always busy, and yet you never do anything in particular; and when you've done it, there's always something else to do, and you can do it if you like, but you'd much better not. . . . And so you've never even *seen* a river before? Well, well!

MOLE Never. And you actually live by it. What a jolly life it sounds.

RAT By it and with it and on it and in it. It's brother and sister to me, and aunts and company, and food and drink, and – naturally – washing. It's my world, and I don't want any other.

MOLE   Isn't it a bit dull at times? Just you and the river and no one else to pass a word with?

RAT   No one else to – no one— Oh well, I mustn't be hard on you. You're new to it. But believe me, my dear young friend, the River Bank is so crowded nowadays that many people are moving away altogether. Otters, kingfishers, dabchicks, moorhens— No one else to— Oh, my dear young friend!

MOLE (*timidly*)   I am afraid you must think me very ignorant.

RAT (*kindly*)   Not at all. Naturally, not being used to it. Look here, what are you doing to-day?

MOLE (*hesitatingly*)   I – I *was* spring-cleaning.

RAT   On a day like this!

MOLE   That's just it. Sometimes I seem to hear a voice within me say 'Whitewash', and then another voice says 'Hang whitewash!' (*Slowly*) And I don't quite know which of the— I don't quite know – I don't qui— Oh, *hang* whitewash!

RAT (*patting him encouragingly*)   That's the spirit. Well, what I was about to suggest was a trifle of lunch on the bank here, and then I'd take you round and introduce you to a few of my friends. Does that appeal to you at all?

MOLE (*ecstatically*)   Does it appeal to me? Does it? Oh my, oh my, oh my!

RAT (*soothingly*)   There, there! You don't want to get *too* excited. It's only just a trifle of lunch. Cold tongue – cold ham – cold chicken – salad – French rolls – cress sandwiches – hard-boiled eggs – bloater paste – tinned peaches – meringues – ginger beer – lemonade – milk – chocolate – oranges— Nothing special – only just—

MOLE (*faintly*) Stop, stop! Oh my, oh my! Oh what a day!

RAT That's all right. You'll feel better soon. Now just you wait here – don't go falling into the river or anything like that – and I'll be back in two minutes with the luncheon-basket.

MOLE (*wiping away the tears*) Oh, Mr Rat, my generous friend, I – I – words fail me for the moment – I – (*he holds out his hand*) – your kindness – that expression, if I caught it correctly, 'luncheon-basket' – a comparative stranger like myself – did I hear you say 'bloater paste?' – you – I— (*He opens his eyes and finds that* RAT *has gone.*) Oh! (*He walks over to a bank of dead leaves and sits down on it.*) Oh, what a day!

> *It is indeed a day. For suddenly the leaves begin to move beneath him, and* MOLE *rises and falls with the motion of a small boat on a choppy sea. A final upheaval dislodges him altogether, the leaves scatter and disclose the recumbent form of* MR BADGER. *Slowly he humps himself into a sitting position and addresses the astonished* MOLE.

BADGER (*gruffly*) Now the *very* next time this happens I shall be exceedingly angry. I have had to speak about it before, and I don't want to speak about it again. But I will *not* have people sitting down on me just as if I were part of the landscape. Now who is it this time? Speak up!

MOLE Oh, please, Mr Badger, it's only me.

BADGER Well, if it's only you, that makes a difference. I don't want to be hard on you. But I put it to you that when an animal is being particularly busy underneath a few leaves, thinking very deeply about things, giving himself up to very serious reflection, he does *not* want to be disturbed. And it *is* disturbing, my little fellow, to have somebody sitting down carelessly on your person, and stretching his legs in an independent sort of way, and—

RAT (*emerging with the lunch*)   Here, Mole, give us a hand with this basket. Hallo! Why, it's Mr Badger!

BADGER   Ah, Ratty, my dear little man, delighted to see you. I was just telling this little fellow—

RAT   By the way, let me introduce you. My friend, Mr Mole.

BADGER   Don't mention it. Any friend of yours, Ratty—

MOLE (*timidly*)   How do you do, Mr Badger? I am very proud to meet you. I'm sure I'm extremely sorry—

BADGER   That's all right, that's all right. Any friend of Ratty's may sit down *where* he likes and *when* he likes, or I'll know the reason why. Well, and what are you two little fellows doing?

RAT   Just having a trifle of lunch. Stay and join us, won't you?

MOLE (*shyly*)   Oh do, Mr Badger! It's a picnic!

He helps RAT *up with the basket.*

BADGER   H'm! Picnics aren't much in my line. Got company coming?

RAT   Only Mole and myself. Unless Toad happens along.

MOLE (*in an ecstatic whisper*)   There's cold tongue – cold chicken – salad – French rolls – cress sandwiches – hard-boiled eggs—

BADGER   Well, if you're sure there's no company. You know, Ratty, I never did like society.

He sits down heavily on the basket, much to MOLE'S *disappointment, who was hoping to get to work at once.*

RAT   Can't say I see much in it myself.

BADGER Sensible animal. And what about your friend Mr Mole?

MOLE Oh, I live a *very* quiet life, Mr Badger. A fieldmouse or two drops in from time to time – perhaps half a dozen of them will come carol-singing at Christmas – but beyond that I hardly see anybody.

BADGER That's right. Ratty, your little friend promises well.

RAT Yes, but you're sitting on the lunch, and we can't—

BADGER (*taking no notice*) He has the right ideas. (*Solemnly*) How different from *one* whom we could mention!

RAT Oh, Toad? Toady's all right.

BADGER (*shaking his head sadly*) Ah me!

MOLE I have heard of the great Mr Toad. He's very rich, isn't he?

RAT Richest animal in these parts, and got one of the nicest houses, though we don't admit as much to Toady. Tudor residence – mullioned windows – bath, hot and cold – and every modern convenience, including carriage sweep. Entertains a lot. Always glad to see you night *or* day. A good fellow, Toady.

BADGER Ah me!

MOLE He must indeed be a very nice animal.

RAT So simple, so good-natured, so affectionate. Perhaps he's not very clever – we can't all be geniuses; and it may be that he is both boastful and conceited. But he has some great qualities has Toady.

MOLE It would be a privilege to make his acquaintance.

RAT Oh, you'll see him all right. He's sure to be along soon.

BADGER And when you see him, my little friend, take warning by him. Society has been his undoing.

RAT   Well, I wouldn't say that. I—

BADGER   If it were not for the desire to shine before his acquaintances, what a much more dependable animal Toad would be! I knew his father. I knew his grandfather. I knew his uncle, the Archdeacon— Ah me!

RAT   Cheer up, old Badger. We'll take him in hand one day and make a better animal of him.

BADGER   Indeed we must. It is a duty I owe to his father. And now that the year is really beginning, and the nights are shorter, and half-way through them one rouses and feels fidgety, and wanting to be up and doing by sunrise, if not before – *you* know—

RAT   *I* know.

BADGER   Well, then, *now* we – you and me and our friend the Mole here, we'll take him in hand and *make* a better animal of him. That is, if we have any more of his nonsense.

RAT   (*nodding*) That's right, Badger. But he's a good fellow, Toady. Doesn't *mean* any harm, you know. Just his way.

MOLE   What *is* his way?

BADGER   You tell him, Rat.

RAT   Crazes. He always has crazes. First it's for sailing, and then it's for punting, and then it's for astronomy, and then it's for carriage horses; and whatever it is, he always has *the* most expensive, and lots of 'em, and knows all about it, or thinks he does, and— Just get up a moment, Badger, you're sitting on the basket.

BADGER   (*not moving*) I knew his father. I knew his uncle the—

RAT   Whatever it is, he must have the best. And then in a week, he's forgotten about it, and started something else.

BADGER Society. That's what's undone him. The craving to shine. (*Solemnly to* MOLE) Very sad, my young friend, very sad. I knew his grandfather.

MOLE (*helpfully*) Dear, dear!

BADGER What his poor father would have said—

TOAD (*off*) Hallo!

RAT (*cheerily*) Hallo, Toady! (*He waves a paw.*) I thought he'd come along soon. You see, he *likes* company.

BADGER (*sadly*) Ah me!

TOAD *comes in boisterously, as full of himself as usual.*

TOAD Hallo, you fellows! This is splendid! Hallo, old Badger! Dear old Ratty! (*He shakes him warmly by the paw.*) Hallo! (*He seizes* MOLE'S *paw and works it up and down.*) And dear old Badger! (*He passes on to* BADGER) How *are* you?

BADGER So-so.

TOAD Splendid, splendid!

RAT My friend, Mr Mole.

TOAD (*going back enthusiastically to* MOLE) How *are* you? (*He shakes his paw vigorously.*) Splendid, eh? That's good. And old Ratty. *And* Badger.

BADGER We were talking about you, my young friend.

TOAD (*spreading himself with delight*) Ah well, the penalty of fame. Eh, Ratty? One gets talked about. One is discussed. One is a topic of conversation. One is speculated about. There it is. One can't help it. Well, Ratty, old man, and how are you?

RAT *I'm* all right. We are just going to have a trifle of lunch. You'd better join us. (*Pulling at the basket again.*) I say, Badger, old man—

TOAD No, no, you all come up to *my* house. Come up to Toad Hall. *I'll* give you lunch, the finest lunch you ever had.

MOLE (*unable to imagine anything superior to* RAT'S *effort*)
But there's cold tongue – cold ham – cold chicken –
salad – French rolls – cress sandwiches – hard-boiled—

TOAD Pooh! Wait till you've seen mine. Ratty knows.
Eh, Ratty? They're quite famous – been referred to in
books. 'Another select little luncheon-party at Toad
Hall.' That sort of thing.

MOLE (*awed*) Oh!

> *He looks anxiously at* RAT, *to whom, after all, he is
> engaged for lunch.*

RAT Now, now, Toad!

BADGER Well, I'll be moving.   *He rises slowly.*

RAT (*getting to the basket at last*) Thanks, old chap.

TOAD That's right. We'll all be moving. (*To* MOLE)
It's only a step to Toad Hall. Jacobean residence – with
bits of Tudor. Finest house on the river. You'll like it.

MOLE (*eagerly*) I'm sure I shall.

BADGER (*to* MOLE) Good-bye, my young friend. We
shall meet again. And before very long, if I'm not
mistaken. Good-bye, Ratty.

RAT Sure you won't stay to lunch.

TOAD But you are coming to lunch with *me*, old Badger.

BADGER (*severely*) Nobody is coming to lunch with
you, Toad. Many a time I have lunched at Toad Hall
with your father; an animal of few words, but of what
an intellect! Ah me! How different from – but I will
not go into that now. Hour after hour, when lunch was
cleared away, we would sit there meditating. I knew
your grandfather, worthy animal that he was. Many a
time have I lunched with him at Toad Hall. Little did
he think, as we sat there reflecting, that one day – but
I shall refer to that later. Good-bye, my unhappy young
friend.   *He goes out heavily.*

MOLE (*anxiously*) Isn't Mr Badger feeling very well?

TOAD (*recovering himself*) Poor old Badger, he gets that way sometimes. No fire, no spirit, no – what's the word – *élan*. Well, well, we can't all have it. Hallo, Ratty, where are you off to?

RAT (*going for it*) The corkscrew.

TOAD (*not moving*) Now, let *me* fetch it. (*To* MOLE) Tell you what, you must come and stay with me. Let me put you up at Toad Hall.

MOLE It's very kind of you, but—

TOAD That's all right. Plenty of room at Toad Hall. Open house for my friends. Always glad to see them. Now what have we got for lunch? (*He assumes the position of host.*) Try one of these sandwiches. (*As* RAT *emerges with the corkscrew.*) Come along, Ratty, try one of these sandwiches. Got the corkscrew? Good. (*To* MOLE) Let me open you one of these bottles. Sit down, Ratty; make yourself comfortable.

RAT (*quietly to* MOLE) Got everything you want?

MOLE Yes, thank you.

RAT That's right. Well, Toady, and what have you been doing lately? Boating? Haven't seen you on the river this last day or two.

TOAD The river! Boating! Bah! Silly boyish amusement. I've given that up *long* ago. Sheer waste of time. No, I've discovered the real thing, the only genuine occupation. I propose to devote the remainder of my life to it. To think of the wasted years that lie behind me, squandered in trivialities!

RAT What's that? Help yourself, Mole.

TOAD Aha, what is it? Come to Toad Hall and you shall see.

MOLE Oh, do let's.

RAT All right, we'll drop in one afternoon.

TOAD Drop in? One afternoon? Nonsense! You're coming to stay. Always welcome, that's my motto. I've had it picked out in green on the front-door mat. 'Always welcome. A home from home.' (*To* MOLE) You'd like to come, wouldn't you?

RAT Sorry, but Mole is staying with *me*.

TOAD Now, you dear good old Ratty, don't begin talking in that stiff and sniffy sort of way, because you know you've got to come. And don't argue; it's the one thing I can't stand. You surely don't mean to stick to your dull fusty old river all your life and just live in a hole in the bank? Come and stay with me, and I'll show you the world.

RAT I don't *want* to see the world. And I *am* going to stick to my old river, *and* live in a hole, just as I've always done. And I'm going to teach Mole all about the river, aren't I, Mole? And Mole is going to stick to me and do as I do, aren't you, Mole?

MOLE (*loyally*) Of course I am. I'll always stick to you, Rat. (*Wistfully*) All the same, it sounds as though it might have been – well, rather fun at Toad Hall.

TOAD Fun? Wait till you see what I've got. I've got the finest— Well, wait till you see it. Pass the sandwiches, Mole, there's a good fellow. (*To* RAT) Seen any of the Wild-Wooders lately?

RAT No.

MOLE Who are the Wild-Wooders?

RAT (*pointing across the river*) They live over there in the Wild Wood. We don't go there very much, we River-Bankers.

MOLE Aren't they – aren't they very nice people in there?

TOAD They daren't show their noses round Toad Hall, that they daren't. I'd soon send them packing.

RAT The squirrels are all right. And the rabbits, of course. And then there's Badger. Dear old Badger. Nobody interferes with *him*. They'd better not.

TOAD And nobody wouldn't interfere with me neither, if I lived there.

MOLE Why, who should?

RAT Well, of course there are others. Weasels and stoats and ferrets and so on. They're all right in a way – I'm very good friends with them—

TOAD So am I.

RAT Pass the time of day when we meet and all that. But they break out sometimes, there's no denying it, and then – well, you really can't trust them, and that's a fact. And if they don't like you, they – well, they show it.

TOAD I wouldn't ask them to Toad Hall, not if they sat up and begged me to. I'm not afraid of them; I just don't like them. They've got no manners, no finesse, if you understand me. Some people are like that, of course. It isn't their fault. You either have finesse, or you haven't. That's how I look at it. Pass the meringues, Mole, there's a good fellow.

> *But* MOLE *is staring beyond* TOAD *at something strange which is approaching – a gaily painted caravan drawn by an old grey horse.*

RAT What is it, Mole?

MOLE Whatever's that?   *They all turn.*

ALFRED (*the horse*) Oh, there you are. I've been look-ing for you everywhere.

TOAD (*excitedly*) Now isn't this lucky? Just at the psycho – psycho – what's the word?

ALFRED (*hopefully*) Encyclopaedia. That is, if you ask *me*.

TOAD I didn't ask you. Ratty, *you* know the word—

ALFRED Introduce me to your friends, won't you? I do get so frightfully left out of it.

TOAD My friends Mr Rat and Mr Mole. This is Alfred.

ALFRED Pleased to meet you. If you're coming my way, you must let me take you. Only I do like a little conversation. (*To* TOAD) Encyclopaedia, that was the word you wanted.

RAT (*sadly*) So this is the latest?

TOAD (*eagerly*) Absolutely the very latest. There isn't a more beautiful one, a more compact one, a more – what's the word?

ALFRED Heavy.

TOAD A more up-to-date one, a more—

RAT So this is the latest craze! I understand. Boating is played out. He's tired of it, and done with it.

ALFRED Don't blame *me*. I wasn't consulted about this at all; but if I had been, I should have said Boats. Stick to Boats.

TOAD My dear old Ratty, you don't understand. Boating – well – a pleasant amusement for the young. I say nothing against it. But there's real life for you – (*he waves a paw at the van*) – in that little cart. The open road, the dusty highway, the heath, the common, the hedgerows, the rolling downs!

ALFRED *And* the ups. However, nobody consults *me*. Nobody minds what *I* think.

TOAD (*warming to it*) Camps, villages, towns, cities! Here to-day, up and off somewhere else to-morrow! Travel, change, interest, excitement! The whole world before you, and a horizon that's always changing.

MOLE (*ecstatically*) Oh my! Oh my!

TOAD And mind, this is the very finest cart of the sort that was ever built, without any exception. Come inside and look at the arrangements, Mole. Planned 'em all myself, I did.

MOLE (*timidly to* RAT) We could just look inside, couldn't we? It wouldn't – wouldn't *mean* anything.

ALFRED (*airily*) Nothing! Nothing!

RAT (*reluctantly*) Oh well, we may as well look at it, now we *are* here. (*Sadly*) Oh, Toady!

TOAD (*leading the way*) All complete! You see – biscuits, potted lobster, sardines – everything you can possibly want. Soda-water here – baccy there—

He shows them into the van, and then his voice dies away.

ALFRED (*to anybody who is listening*) That's right. Go inside and enjoy yourselves! Talk to each other, tell each other little stories, but don't ask *me* to join in the conversation. Encyclopaedia – that was the word he wanted. *I* could have told him.

TOAD (*emerging*) Bacon, jam, cards, dominoes – you'll find that nothing whatever has been forgotten.

ALFRED (*with feeling*) I've noticed it.

TOAD Well, what do you think of it, Mole?

MOLE It's lovely!

TOAD Glad you like it. What about starting this afternoon?

RAT (*slowly*) I beg your pardon, did I overhear you say something about 'starting'?

ALFRED Starting – that's what he said. I'm not even consulted.

TOAD Come on, we'll just put the rest of the lunch inside – come on, Mole, give us a hand—

MOLE (*torn between the two of them*) Oh, Ratty!

TOAD Come on, Ratty, old fellow. This is the real life for a gentleman. Talk about your old river!

>*He begins packing up the lunch.*

RAT I *don't* talk about my river. You *know* I don't, Toad. . . . But I *think* about it. I think about it – all the time.

MOLE (*squeezing* RAT'S *paw*) I'll do whatever you like, Ratty. We won't go. I want to stay with *you*. And – learn about your river.

RAT No, no, we'd better see it out now. It wouldn't be safe for him to go off by himself. It won't take long – his crazes never do.

ALFRED When *I* was young, it was considered bad manners to whisper, and leave people out of conversations. (*In a loud conversational voice*) My own view – since asked – of the climatic conditions, is that the present anticyclonic disturbance in the—

TOAD Here, give us a hand, Mole. . . . That's right. . . . All aboard? Here, we're forgetting the corkscrew. Will you get it? (MOLE *trots back for it*.) Don't bother. *I'll*— Oh, you've got it. Good! Now then, are we all ready?

ALFRED No.

TOAD You get up there, Mole. (MOLE *sits on the shaft on one side of the caravan*.) You on the other side, Ratty? Or would you rather— (RAT *goes to the horse's head*.) Oh, are *you* going to lead him? I will, if you like. Sure you don't mind? Right, then I'll get up here. Now then, right away! *They start off*.

ALFRED (*to* RAT) You mark my words. No good will come of this. But don't blame *me*. That's all. Don't blame *me* afterwards. Psychological – that was the word he wanted. Not encyclopaedia. I thought it seemed funny somehow. Psychological. *The caravan goes out.*

*

It grows dark. A thunderstorm, you would say, is brewing. In the darkness scuffing noises can be heard; breathings. It becomes lighter, and now we can see. The WILD-WOODERS *are here!* FERRETS, WEASELS, STOATS *perform weird evolutions as they chant their terrible war-song:*

Toad! Toad! Down with Toad!
Down with the popular, successful Toad!
The three CHIEF CONSPIRATORS *form a mystic circle in the middle and utter this horrid incantation:*

CHIEF FERRET:
O may his bathroom cistern spring a leak!

CHIEF WEASEL:
On Sunday morning may his collar squeak!

CHIEF STOAT:
May all his laces tie themselves in knots,

CHIEF FERRET:
And may his fountain-pen make frequent blots!

CHIEF WEASEL:
May he forget to wind his watch at night,

CHIEF STOAT:
And may his dancing-pumps be *much* too tight!
                              They dance solemnly.

THE FERRETS:
Every ill which Toad inherits
Will be welcomed by the Ferrets.

ALL:
Down with Toad! Down with Toad!

THE WEASELS:
  Day and night the elder Weasels
  Hope that he will have the measles.
ALL:
  Down with Toad! Down with Toad!

THE STOATS:
  How the happy little Stoats
  Laugh when he is off his oats!
ALL:
  Down with Toad! Down with Toad!
  Toad! Toad! Down with Toad!
  Down with the popular, successful Toad!

> *It grows dark again. The* WILD-WOODERS *can still be
> heard chanting their diabolical refrain, but they can no
> longer be seen. There is a loud clap of thunder; it is day-
> light again; the* WILD-WOODERS *have vanished. Then
> the 'poop-poop' of a motor-car is heard, followed by a
> loud crash. Suddenly in comes a violently-excited* ALFRED,
> *the broken ends of the shafts attached to him, but no
> caravan.* MOLE *follows.*

MOLE (*soothingly to* ALFRED) There, there! . . . There,
  there! (*But* ALFRED *refuses to 'there, there!' He careers
  round the stage, pursued by the conciliatory* MOLE.) There,
  there! It's all right, Alfred. (*Very reassuringly*) It's all
  right.

> RAT *comes in, supporting a dazed* TOAD.

RAT (*turning and shaking his fist at something*) You villains!
  You scoundrels, you highwaymen, you – you—
ALFRED (*still gryatiug*) Road-hogs. That's the word.
  Always come to me if you want the right word. Road-
  hogs.

RAT You road-hogs! I'll have the law of you! Rushing about the country at fifty miles an hour! I'll write to all the papers about you! I'll take you through all the Courts (*Turning anxiously to* TOAD) How are you feeling now, Toady? Mole, come and give us a hand with poor old Toad. I'm afraid he's pretty bad.

MOLE (*catching up* ALFRED *at last*) There, there! That's all right now, isn't it? (*Going to* RAT) Poor old Toad!
He takes his other arm, and together he and RAT *conduct the dazed one to a grassy bank, and sit him gently down.*

ALFRED I said that no good would come of it, and now you see. A cataclysm – that's what the whole thing's been.

RAT (*anxiously*) Speak to us, Toady, old man! How is it?

TOAD (*staring in front of him with a rapt expression*) Poop-poop! . . . Poop-poop! . . . Poop-poop!

MOLE What's he saying?

RAT I *think* he thinks he's the motor-car.

TOAD Poop-poop!

MOLE (*soothingly*) It's all right, Mr Toad. It's all right now.

RAT We'll make 'em sit up, Toad. We'll have the law of 'em. We'll get you another little cart – we'll make 'em pay for it.

ALFRED Another! Oh, thank you, thank you, not at all, don't mention it, only too delighted.

TOAD Poop-poop! . . . (*Raptly he speaks*) Glorious, stirring sight! The poetry of motion! The *real* way to travel! The *only* way to travel! Here to-day – in the middle of next week to-morrow! Villages skipped, towns and cities jumped – always somebody else's horizon. Oh bliss, oh rapture! Oh poop-poop!

RAT Oh, stop being an ass, Toad!

TOAD (*dreamily*) And to think that I never knew! All those wasted years that lie behind me, I never knew, never even dreamt. But now that I know, now that I fully realize – ah, now! Oh what a flowery track lies spread before me henceforth! What savoury dust-clouds shall spring up behind me as I speed on my reckless way, what luscious and entrancing smells. What carts I shall fling carelessly into the ditch in the wake of my magnificent onset. Horrid little carts – common carts – canary-coloured carts!

RAT Now, look here, Toad, pull yourself together. We'll go to the police-station, and see if they know anything about that motor-car, and then we'll lodge a complaint against the owners, and we'll go to a wheelwright's and have the cart fetched and mended and put to rights, and we'll—

TOAD Police-station? Complaint! *Me* complain of that beautiful, that heavenly vision which has been vouchsafed me? *Mend* the *cart*? I've done with carts for ever. Horrid little carts, common carts, canary-coloured carts!

MOLE (*hopelessly*) What are we to do with him?

TOAD Oh Ratty! Oh, my good friend Mr Mole! You can't think how obliged I am to you for coming with me on this glorious trip. I wouldn't have gone without you, and then I might never have seen that – that swan, that star, that thunderbolt. I might never have heard that entrancing sound, nor smelt that bewitching smell! I owe it all to you, my dear, my very dear friends.

RAT (*sadly*) I see what it is. I recognize the symptoms. He is in the grip of a new craze.

Faintly the FERRETS *and the* STOATS *and the* WEASELS
are heard singing:

> Down with Toad! Down with Toad!
> Down with the popular, successful Toad!

TOAD (*raptly*) Poop-poop!

RAT (*to* MOLE)   Well, come along. Let's get him home.

MOLE   Come on, Alfred.

ALFRED (*sadly*)   One of the most distressing cases which
has come under our notice. Very sad! Very sad!

TOAD   Poop-poop!

> *They trudge off. As soon as they are gone, the Bank is alive
> again with the* WILD-WOODERS, *who burst into mocking
> laughter.*

Act Two

*

SCENE I · THE WILD WOOD

The middle of the Wild Wood. It is an awesome place in the moonlight, with the snow thick upon the ground; cold, silent, threatening. Yet not altogether silent, that is the worst of it. You feel that there are hidden watchers behind the trees, waiting to jump out at you; you hear, or seem to hear, their stealthy movements. There is a sudden rustling . . . and then silence. A twig cracks. Somebody is breathing . . . .

Now at last we can recognize somebody. It is TOAD, *in motoring gloves and goggles, coming anxiously through the trees, with many a sudden stop and furtive glance over his shoulder. We can hear, and he hears too, a murmur of unseen voices, which rises in a sort of chant until at last we can distinguish the words.*

CHORUS OF WILD-WOODERS:

Toad! Toad! Down with Toad!
Down with the popular, successful Toad!

TOAD (*alarmed*)   W-what's that?
                              Mocking laughter answers him.
Pah!   *Dead silence.*
I said 'Pah!' (*Nervously*) A-and 'Bah!' (*Loudly*) Bah!
(*There is an echoing 'Bah'.*) What's that? (*Again the echo of the last word comes back to him, and he laughs, but a little*

25

uneasily.) Silly of me. Just an echo. Something to do with the acoustics. I must tell Rat. He'd be interested.

CHORUS (*softly*):

> Toad! Toad! Down with Toad!
> Down with the gallant and courageous Toad!

TOAD (*sharply*)   Who said that?
> *Mocking laughter answers him.*
I can see you.   *Dead silence.*
Very funny, aren't you? I suppose you think I'm afraid? (*Loudly*) I said I suppose you think I'm *afraid*? (*There is an echoing 'afraid'*.) There you are, it's nothing. Just an echo. Listen. (*Hand to mouth*) Rat! (*Dead silence*.) Perhaps it doesn't work sometimes. Something to do with the direction of the wind. I'll try again. (*Very loudly*) RAT!

A SOLEMN VOICE   Mole!
> *And then a burst of laughter.*

CHORUS (*in quick, business-like time*):

> Toad! Toad! Down with Toad!
> Down with the terrified and timorous Toad!

TOAD   C-c-come and do it! C-come and do it if you dare. (*The mocking laughter again*.) Yes, that's all you can do – laugh. Any one can laugh. Ha-ha-ha-ha-ha! Very funny, isn't it?

A VOICE   Where are you going, Toad?

TOAD   Never you mind where I'm going. I'm going to see Badger, that's where I'm going. (*More confidently as he thinks of* BADGER.) My *friend*, Mr Badger. I'm calling on my old and valued boon-companion, the fierce and terrible Badger!   *Loud laughter.*

A LOW VOICE Where are you going to, my pretty Toad?

A HIGH VOICE Just a little way down the road.

A LOW VOICE Why are you wearing your bonnet and shawl?

A HIGH VOICE Because I am paying an evening call.

A LOW VOICE Knock at the door, for here's the house.

A HIGH VOICE Ah! Good evening, Mr Mouse!

There is another burst of laughter.

A VOICE Badger doesn't live here, Toad!

TOAD (*desperately, greeting an imaginary friend*) Yes, he does, there he is. Ah, my dear Badger, how *are* you? No, not at all. Yes, delighted, quite so, no, yes, not in the least. Fancy! Ha-ha! Well, yes, just a little walk through the wood. Oh, do you think so? And you're looking splendid yourself. Never saw you looking fiercer. (*Loudly*) I said *fiercer*! (*As he goes off*) This way, my dear Badger!

A VOICE Good-bye, Toad!

A HIGH VOICE (*answering*) Good-bye!

A VOICE Good-bye, Mouse.

A SQUEAKY VOICE (*answering*) Good-bye!

There is a last shout of laughter as TOAD *disappears.*

CHORUS (*softly*):

Toad! Toad! Down with Toad!
Chilblains and Mumps to the Miserable Toad!
Toad! Toad! Down with Toad!
Frostbite and Hiccups to the Miserable Toad!

The chant goes on, a murmur of unseen voices, whose words we can no longer distinguish. In a little while we can hear nothing, and yet it seems that at any moment we shall hear something. No wonder that MOLE, *limping through the trees, keeps looking over his shoulder.*

MOLE (*hopefully*) Ratty! (*In sudden panic*) What's that? (*The movements stop.*) Pooh! It's nothing! *I'm* not frightened! . . . I do wish Ratty were here. He's so comforting, is Ratty. Or the brave Mr Toad. *He'd* frighten them all away. (*He seems to hear the sound of mocking laughter.*) What's that? (*He looks round anxiously.*) Ratty always said, 'Don't go into the Wild Wood.' That's what he always said. 'Not by yourself,' he said. 'It isn't safe,' he said. 'We *never* do,' he said. That's what Ratty said. But I thought I knew better. There he was, dear old Rat, dozing in front of the fire, and I thought if I just slipped out, just to see what the Wild Wood was like— (*He breaks off suddenly and darts round, fearing an attack from behind. There is nothing.*) I should be safer up against a tree. Why didn't I think of that before? (*He settles himself at the foot of a tree.*) Ratty would have thought of it, he's so wise. Oh, Ratty, I wish you were here! It's so much more friendly with two!   *His head droops on his chest.*

A VOICE (*from far off*) Moly! Moly!

MOLE (*waking up suddenly*) What's that?

A VOICE Moly!

MOLE (*frightened*) Who is it?

A VOICE Moly! Moly! Moly! Where are you? It's me – it's old Rat!

RAT *appears; a lantern in his hand, a couple of pistols in his belt, and a cudgel over his shoulder.*

MOLE (*almost in tears*) Oh, Rat! Oh, Rat!

RAT (*patting him on the back*) There, there, there!

MOLE Oh, Ratty, I've been so frightened, you can't think.

RAT *I* know, *I* know. You shouldn't have gone and done it, Mole. I did my best to keep you from it. We River-Bankers hardly ever come, except in couples.

MOLE But *you've* come by *yourself*. Ah, but then that's because you're so brave.

RAT It isn't just bravery, it's knowing. There are a hundred things you have to know, which we understand about, and you don't as yet. I mean passwords and signs, and sayings which have power and effect, and plants you carry in your pocket, and verses you repeat backwards, and dodges and tricks you practise; all simple enough if you know them, but if you don't, you'll find yourself in trouble. Of course if you're Badger, it's different.

MOLE Surely the brave Mr Toad wouldn't mind coming here by himself?

RAT (*laughing*) Old Toad? He wouldn't show his face here alone, not for a whole hatful of guineas, Toad wouldn't.

MOLE Oh, Rat! It is comforting to hear somebody laugh again.

RAT Poor old Mole! What a rotten time you've had. Never mind, we'll soon be home now. How would a little mulled ale strike you – after you've got into slippers, of course? I made the fire up specially.

MOLE You think of everything, Ratty.

RAT Well, shall we start?

MOLE Oh, Ratty. I don't know how to tell you, and I'm afraid you'll never want me for a companion again, but I can't, I simply *can't* go all that way now.

RAT Tired?

MOLE Aching all over. Oh, Ratty, do forgive me. I feel as if I must just sit here for ever and ever and ever, and

I'm not a bit frightened now you're with me – and – and I think I want to go to sleep.

RAT That's all right. But we can't stop *here*. (*He looks round about him.*) Suppose we go and dig in that mound there, and see if we can't make some sort of a shelter out of the snow and the wind, and have a good rest. And then start for home a bit later on. How's that?

MOLE (*meekly*) Just as you like.

RAT Come on, then.

He leads the way to the mound, and MOLE, *following, trips up suddenly and falls over with a squeal.*

MOLE Oh, my leg! Oh, my poor shin! Oo!

RAT Poor old Mole, you don't seem to be having much luck to-day, do you? What is it? Hurt your shin? Let's have a look at it.

MOLE I must have tripped over a stump or something. Oh my! oh my!

RAT It's a very clean cut. That was never done by a stump. Looks like the sharp edge of something metal. Funny!

MOLE Well, never mind what done it. It hurts just the same whatever done it.

RAT Wait a moment. *He begins scratching in the snow.*

MOLE What is it?

RAT I thought so!

MOLE (*still nursing his leg*) What *is* it?

RAT Come and see.

MOLE (*hobbling up*) Hullo, a door-scraper! How very careless of somebody!

RAT But don't you see what it means?

MOLE (*sitting down again and rubbing his shin*) Of course I see what it means. It means that some *very* forgetful person has left his door-scraper lying about in the middle of the Wild Wood just where it's sure to trip everybody up. Somebody ought to write to him about it.

RAT   Oh, Mole, how stupid you are. (*He begins scratching busily again.*) There! What's that?

MOLE (*examining it closely*)   It looks like a door-mat.

RAT   It *is* a door-mat. And what does *that* tell you?

MOLE   Nothing, Rat, nothing. Who ever heard of a door-mat telling any one anything? They simply don't do it. They are not that sort at all. They—what have you found *now*?

   RAT, *still at it, has now disclosed a solid-looking little door, dark green, with a brass plate on it.*

RAT (*proudly*)   There! (*He fetches the lantern and holds it up to the plate.*) What do you read there?

MOLE (*awestruck*)   'Mr Badger. Seventh Wednesdays'. . . . Rat!

RAT (*proudly*)   What do you think of *that*?

MOLE   Rat, you're a wonder, that's what you are! I see it all now. You argued it out step by step from the moment when I fell and cut my shin, and you looked at the cut, and your majestic mind said to itself, 'Doorscaper'. Did it stop there? No. Your powerful brain went on working. It said to itself—

RAT (*impatiently*)   Yes, yes, well now let's—

MOLE (*going on sleepily and happily*)   Your powerful brain said to itself, 'Where there's a scraper, there must be a mat.'

RAT   Quite so. And now—

MOLE
'I have noticed before,' said the wise Mr Rat,
'That where there's a scraper there must be a mat.'
And did you stop *there*? No. Your intellect still went on

working. It said grandly to itself, 'Where there's a door-mat there must be a door.'

RAT   Exactly. And now that we've found it—

MOLE

Said the wise Mr Rat, 'I have noticed before,
That where there's a door-mat there must be a door.'
You know, Rat, you're simply wasted here amongst
us fellows. If I only had your head—

RAT   But as you haven't, I suppose you are going to sit
on the snow and *talk* all night. Now wake up a bit
and hang on to this bell-pull, while I hammer.

MOLE (*sleepily*)   Oh, all right!

Said the wise Mr Rat, 'I have often heard tell
That where there's a bell-pull there *must* be a bell.'

He hangs on to the bell-pull, while RAT *hammers on the
door with his cudgel. Down in* MR BADGER'S *house a
deep-toned bell responds.*

SCENE 2 · BADGER'S HOUSE

BADGER'S *underground home. The room which we see is one of those delightful mixtures of hall, kitchen, drawing-room, dining-room, larder and pantry. In the middle of the room, says Mr Kenneth Grahame, but we shall probably put it to one side, stands a long table of plain boards on trestles, with benches drawn up to it. There is a big open fireplace with high-backed settles on each side; an arm-chair in which the owner can read* The Times, *and is now so doing. The floor is brick; from the rafters hang hams, nets of onions and bundles of herbs. In short, a place where heroes can feast after victory, harvesters keep their Harvest Home with mirth and song, and two or three friends sit about as they please in comfort and content. There are three doors, labelled* FRONT DOOR, BACK DOOR, *and* STUDY. *At a knocking on the Back Door a convulsion passes over* The Times; *at a second knocking it stands on end; and at a third* MR BADGER *comes out from behind the leading article. Grumbling to himself, for his after-supper nap has been disturbed, he goes to the door.*

BADGER (*opening the door*) Well, well, well, what is it, what is it?

A collection of FIELD-MICE, *half a dozen of them in red mufflers, stand nervously shuffling at the entrance.*

FIRST FIELD-MOUSE (*huskily*) Oh, please, Mr Badger, did you want any carols?

BADGER Any *what*? Speak up!

FIRST FIELD-MOUSE (*swallowing*) Carols.

BADGER Let's have a look at them.

SECOND FIELD-MOUSE (*striking up*) 'Good King Wenceslas looked out—'

BADGER Oh, I thought you said carrots. Run along, all of you. Time you were in bed.

SECOND FIELD-MOUSE 'Good King Wenceslas looked out—'

BADGER And if you come round disturbing *me* again, *you'll* have to look out. Now then, off you go.

FIRST FIELD-MOUSE Oh, please, Mr Badger, we always used to sing carols to Mr Mole, and he used to ask us in, and give us hot drinks, and supper too sometimes.

SECOND FIELD-MOUSE (*proudly*) We had steak-and-kidney pudding once.

FIRST FIELD-MOUSE That's right, sir.

SECOND FIELD-MOUSE Real steak-and-kidney pudding with kidney in it.

FIRST FIELD-MOUSE That was Mr Mole, sir. Down at Mole End. Always asked us in, Mr Mole did.

BADGER Ah! Mole did, did he? And Mole is a very sensible young animal. I have great hopes of Mole. Well, run away now, but come back in twenty minutes, when I'm not so busy, and perhaps I'll let you sing me the – what did you call it?

FIELD-MICE (*eagerly*) Carol.

BADGER Carol. I thought you said carrot. Well, then, you can sing the one that Mr Mole liked, and if I like it too, I won't say that perhaps there won't be a bit of hot something for one or two of you, the ones that don't snuffle, that is, and—

FIELD-MICE Oh, thank you, Mr Badger.

BADGER Now then, run along, there's good children.

(*They run along.*) So Mole likes carols, does he? (*He goes back to his chair, and covers his face up again.*) Likes carols, does he? (*He breathes heavily.*) Carols. . . . Thought he said carrots.

> *He snores. . . . But he is not to sleep long. This time it is the front door bell which rings; again – and again. There is a hammering too, at the door. Very much annoyed,* BADGER *gets to his feet.*

BADGER   *All* right, *all* right, *all* right! What is it, who is it? (*He opens the front door.*) Speak up!

RAT   Hallo, Badger! It's me, Rat, and my friend Mole, and we've lost our way in the snow, and Mole's that tired you never did.

BADGER   Well, well, well! Rat and his friend Mole! (*He brings them in.*) Come along in, both of you, at once. Why, you must be perished! Well I never! Lost in the snow! And your friend that tired! Well, well! And in the Wild Wood at this time of night! (*He pats their heads paternally.*) I'm afraid you've been up to some of your pranks again, Ratty. But come along in. There's a good fire here, and supper and everything.

MOLE   (*as he sees the supper-table*)   Oo, I say!

> *He nudges the* RAT *in an anticipatory sort of way.*

BADGER   Now what will you do first? Toast your toes a bit? (*He removes* The Times.) I was just glancing at the paper. Or supper now, and toast your toes afterwards? It's all ready. I was expecting one or two friends might drop in.

MOLE (*shyly*)   I think I should like supper at once, please, Mr Badger.

BADGER   That's right, Mole. Sensible animal. And what about you, Rat?

RAT (*who is standing with his back to the fire, as an old friend should*) Just as you like. Fine old place this, isn't it, Mole?

MOLE (*already among the plates*) Grand.

He sits down to it. RAT *fetches himself a sandwich and gets his back to the fire again.* BADGER, *in an armchair, beams upon them kindly.*

BADGER (*to* RAT) Won't your friend try some of those pickles?

RAT Try a pickle, Mole.

MOLE (*his mouth full*) Thanks. *He helps himself.*

BADGER (*solemnly, after a silence broken only by the noise of eating*) I've been wanting to see you fellows, because I have heard very grave reports of our mutual friend, Toad.

RAT (*sadly*) Oh, Toad! *He shakes his head.*

MOLE (*as sympathetically as he can with a mouth full of pickles*) Tut-tut-tut.

BADGER Is his case as hopeless as one has heard?

RAT Going from bad to worse – that's all you can say about him, isn't it, Mole?

MOLE (*nodding busily*) 'M! (*Swallowing hastily.*) That's all.

RAT Another smash-up only last week, and a bad one. You see, since he's got this motor craze, he will insist on driving himself, and he's hopelessly incapable. If he'd only employ a decent, steady, well-trained animal, pay him good wages and leave everything to him, he'd get on all right. But no; he's convinced he's the greatest driver ever, and nobody can teach him anything. And so it goes on.

MOLE And so it goes on.

BADGER (*gloomily*) And so it goes on! (*After a pause*) How many has he had?

RAT Cars or smashes? Oh well, it's the same thing with Toad. The last was the seventh.

MOLE He's been in hospital three times, and as for the fines he's had to pay—

RAT Toad's rich, we all know, but he's not a millionaire. Killed or ruined, it will be one or the other with Toad.

BADGER Alas, alas! I knew his father, I knew his grandfather. Many's the time— (*A sob chokes him.*) Alas, poor witless animal!

MOLE (*still busy*) You really ought to try a slice of this beef, Rat.

RAT No, thanks, really.

MOLE Don't know when I've tasted better.

RAT (*to* BADGER) Oughtn't we to *do* something? We're his friends.

BADGER Yes, you're right. The hour has come.

MOLE (*anxiously*) What hour?

BADGER Whose hour, you should say. Toad's hour. The hour of Toad.

RAT (*quietly*) Well done, Badger. I knew you'd feel that way too.

MOLE (*firmly*) *We'll* teach him to be a sensible Toad.

BADGER At any moment another new and exceptionally powerful motor-car will arrive at Toad Hall for approval or return. We must be up and doing ere it is too late.

RAT That's right, Badger. We'll rescue the poor unhappy animal! We'll convert him! He'll be the most converted Toad that ever was before we've finished with him.

BADGER The first step is to get him here and reason with him. You know how it is. In the present weather, I don't go about much. Naturally.

RAT Of course not.

MOLE Of course not.

BADGER But once Toad is here—

RAT How to get him, that's the problem—

BADGER (*gravely*) Let us apply our minds to it.

> *They apply their minds. Absent-mindedly, while thinking,*
> MOLE *helps himself to beef. Suddenly the bell rings loudly.*

BADGER Whoever's that?

> *He shuffles off to the door, and as he opens it,* TOAD *falls*
> *into his arms, panting with fear.*

RAT (*in surprise*) Why, it's Toad!

MOLE Hallo, Toad, you ought to try some of this beef!

RAT Why, what's the matter? (TOAD, *supported by*
BADGER, *falls limply into a chair and sits there panting.*)
Another accident? (TOAD *shakes his head.*) That's some-
thing.

TOAD (*still panting a little*) Ah, Ratty, my dear old Ratty,
and my good friend Mole, how badly I seemed to need
your help just now! What would I not have given to
have had you by my side. As it was, I had to do the
best I could without you. Fortunately it was enough.
But as you see, it has exhausted me somewhat.

RAT What's happened? Wild-Wooders?

TOAD (*warming to it*) An unfortunate breakdown in my
car – a loose nut, some trifling mishap – left me
stranded at the edge of the wood, far from home. I
bethought me of my good friend Mr Badger; he would
lend me a sleeping suit and put me up for the night.
As I came whistling through the wood, recking naught
of danger, I was suddenly seized upon by a gang of
rascally ferrets. I set about them light-heartedly – at
the most there were no more than a dozen of them –
when suddenly, to my horror, they were reinforced

by a posse of scoundrelly weasels. It was then, Ratty –
and my dear friend Mole – that I wished I had your
assistance. Twelve of the rascals, yes (*he is now standing
up, legs straddled, and enjoying himself immensely*), but
twenty-four of them is a different matter. If only you
and Mole could have taken a couple of them off my
hands, there might have been a different story to tell.
As it was, a rearguard action was forced upon me. Step
by step—(*He realizes a faint hostile something in the air, particularly from the direction of* BADGER. *He goes on less
confidently.*) Step by step— (*He looks from one to the other,
hoping for a little encouragement, but the atmosphere is now
really terrible; nobody could tell even the simplest story in it.
He makes a last desperate effort.*) Step by step—

BADGER (*solemnly*) Won't you sit down again, Toad?

TOAD (*meekly*) Thank you.

RAT Would you care to be nearer the fire?

TOAD (*faintly*) No, thank you.

MOLE Let me put your gloves down for you.

TOAD It's all right, thank you.

BADGER (*to* RAT) The moment has come, I think,
don't you?

RAT I think so.

BADGER (*to* MOLE) You agree?

MOLE Yes.   *He sighs.*

TOAD (*uneasily*) I say, you fellows, what's all this—
    He catches BADGER'S *eye and is silent again.*

BADGER (*solemnly*) Toad! I knew your father, worthy
animal that he was; I knew your grandfather. It was
also my privilege to be slightly acquainted with your
uncle, the Archdeacon; of that I shall speak further
directly. The question I wish to ask you now is this. At
the beginning of the breathless story of adventure to

which we have just been listening, you mentioned (*he
pauses dramatically*) a motor-car. You implied further
that this motor-car had suddenly lost its efficiency. Am
I right in supposing that just at this moment your nar-
rative hovered for an instant on the confines of truth?

TOAD (*sulkily*)   What do you mean?

RAT   Really, Toad, he couldn't have put it more plainly.

BADGER   I asked you, Toad, if it is indeed a fact that
your eighth motor-car is now in as fragmentary a condition as the previous seven?

TOAD (*sulkily*)   I had a little accident.

BADGER   Thank you. (*To* RAT) Then I think that in
that case we may begin the treatment?

RAT   Yes, I think so.

BADGER (*to* MOLE)   You agree?

MOLE   Yes.

TOAD   I say, you fellows—

BADGER   Toad! (TOAD *looks at him.*) Rise from your
chair a moment. (TOAD *rises.*) Rat, Mole, may I trouble
you a moment? (*He indicates that he wants* TOAD'S *chair
in a position where he can be harangued better. They rise to
move it.*) Thank you. . . . There, I think. . . . Perhaps
just a trifle more to the left. . . . Thank you. Toad!

He points to the chair and TOAD *meekly creeps into it.*

RAT (*kindly*)   This is all for your good, Toady old man.

BADGER   Now then, first of all take those ridiculous
goggles off.

TOAD (*plucking up courage*)   Shan't! What is the meaning
of this gross outrage? I demand an instant explanation.

BADGER   Take them off then, you two.

RAT (*as* TOAD *looks like showing fight*)   It's all for your
own good, Toady old man. We've been talking it over
for hours. Might as well take it quietly.

MOLE We don't like doing it, Toad, really we don't. It's only because we are so fond of you.

They remove the goggles.

BADGER That is better. It was thus that your father knew you. It was thus that your grandfather, had he survived a year or two longer, would have known you. Now then, Toad. You've disregarded all the warnings we've given you, you've gone on squandering the money your father left you, and you're getting us animals a bad name in the district by your furious driving and your smashes and your rows with the police. We have decided, my friend Ratty here and Mole and I, that it is time we saved you from yourself. I am going to make one more effort to bring you to reason. You will come with me into my study, and there you will hear some facts about yourself. I say the study, because on second thoughts I have decided, for the sake of your revered grandfather, to spare you the pain of a public reproof. Come!

TOAD (*meekly*) Yes, Badger. Thank you, Badger.

They go out together.

RAT That's no good! Talking to Toad will never cure him. He'll *say* anything.

MOLE Yes.   *He sighs.*

RAT We must *do* something.

MOLE Yes.   *He sighs again.*

RAT (*looking at him suddenly*) What's the matter, old fellow? You seem melancholy. Too much beef?

MOLE (*bravely*) Oh, no, it isn't that. It was just – no, never mind, I shall be all right directly.

He wipes away a tear.

RAT Why, whatever is it?

MOLE Nothing, Ratty, nothing. I was just admiring

Badger's great big house and comparing it with my own little home, which – which I haven't seen lately – just comparing it, you know, and thinking about it – and thinking about it – and comparing it. Not meaning to, you know. Just happening to – think about it.

RAT (*remorsefully*) Oh, Mole!

MOLE (*in a sudden burst*) I know it's a shabby, dingy little place; not like your cosy quarters, or Toad's beautiful Hall, or Badger's great house – but it was my own little home – and I was fond of it – and I went away and forgot all about it – and since we've been down here it's all been coming back to me – perhaps it's the pickles – *I* always had Military Pickles too – I shall be better soon – I don't know what you'll think of me.

RAT (*patting him on the back*) Poor old Mole! Been rather an exciting day, hasn't it? And then the same sort of pickles. Tell me about Mole End. We might go and pay it a visit to-morrow if you've nothing better to do.

MOLE It wouldn't be fine enough for *you*. You're used to great big places and fine houses. I noticed directly we came in how you stood with your back to the fire so grandly and easily, just as if it were nothing to you.

RAT Well, *you* tucked into the beef, old chap.

MOLE Did I?

RAT Rather! Made yourself quite at home. I said to myself at once, 'Mole is used to going out,' I said. 'Week-end parties at big country houses,' I said, 'that's nothing to Mole,' I said.

MOLE (*eagerly*) Did you really, Ratty?

RAT Oh, rather! Spotted it at once.

MOLE Of course there *were* features about Mole End which made it rather – rather—

RAT Rather a feature?

MOLE Yes. The statuary. I'd picked up a bit of statuary here and there – you'd hardly think how it livened the place up. Garibaldi, the Infant Samuel, and Queen Victoria – dotted about in odd corners. It had a very pleasing effect, my friends used to tell me.

RAT (*heartily*) I should like to have seen that, Mole, I should indeed. That must have been very striking.

MOLE It was just about now that they used to come carol-singing.

RAT Garibaldi – and the others?

MOLE The field-mice.

RAT Oh yes, of course.

MOLE Quite an institution they were. They never passed me over – always came to Mole End last, and I gave them hot drinks, and supper sometimes, when I could afford it.

RAT Yes, I remember now hearing about it, and what a fine place Mole End was.

MOLE (*wistfully*) Did you? . . . It wasn't very big.

RAT Between ourselves, I don't much care about these big places. Cosy and tasteful, that's what I always heard about Mole End.

MOLE (*squeezing* RAT'S *paw*) You're a good friend, Ratty. I like being with you.

RAT Good old Mole!

They are happily silent together. Suddenly, faint and far-off and sweet, a carol can be heard . . . 'the carol that Mr Mole liked'.

MOLE There they are!

They listen raptly. When it is over they give a little sigh: for it is time now to get back to business. The door opens and BADGER *comes in, leading by the paw a very dejected* TOAD.

BADGER (*kindly*) Sit down there, Toad. (TOAD *sits down*.) My friends, I am pleased to inform you that Toad has at last seen the error of his ways. He is truly sorry for his misguided conduct in the past, and he has undertaken to give up motor-cars entirely and for ever in the future. I have his solemn promise to that effect.

MOLE (*eagerly*) Oh, Toad, I *am* glad!

RAT (*doubtfully*) H'm!

BADGER There is only one thing which remains to be done. Toad, I want you solemnly to repeat before your friends here what you fully admitted to me in the study just now. First, you are sorry for what you have done and see the folly of it all?

> *There is an anxious silence.*

TOAD (*suddenly*) No! I'm *not* sorry. And it wasn't folly at all. It was simply glorious!

BADGER (*horrified*) What?

MOLE Toady!

RAT I thought so.

BADGER You back-sliding animal, didn't you tell me just now in there—

TOAD Oh yes, yes, in *there*. I'd have said anything in *there*. You're so eloquent, dear Badger, and so moving, and so convincing, and put all your points so frightfully well – you can do what you like with me in *there*. But, thinking it over out *here*. I see that I am not a bit sorry really, so it's no earthly good saying I am; now is it?

BADGER Then you don't promise never to touch a motor-car again?

TOAD Of course I don't. On the contrary, I faithfully promise that the very first motor-car I see – Poop-poop, off I go in it!

RAT (*to* MOLE)   I told you so.

BADGER   Very well then. Since you won't yield to persuasion, we'll try what force can do. I feared it would come to this all along. You'll stay with me, Toad, until a cure has been effected. My friends, Rat and Mole, will also stay with me and help me to look after you. It's going to be a tedious business, but we will see it out. (*He takes down a large key from the wall, and picking up the lantern leads the way to the guest-chamber.*) Bring him along.

They bring him along. The procession goes slowly, and on TOAD'S *part reluctantly, out.*

Badger's home on a spring morning some weeks later.
MR BADGER *is in an arm-chair, with his feet on another
reading a newspaper, and paying no attention whatever to*
TOAD, *who is in the paroxysms of another attack.* TOAD
(*poor fellow*) *has arranged three chairs in a hopeful rep-
resentation of a motor-car. He sits on the front one, grasp-
ing an imaginary wheel, changing imaginary gears, and
making appropriate noises. A sudden (imaginary) block
in the traffic pulls him up sharply, though his 'Hi, look
ahead there!' averts an accident. He gets off and winds up
his engine, then lifts the bonnet and peers in. In a little while
he is off again; but now a real accident upsets him. The
chairs are strewn about and* TOAD *lies panting in the
wreckage.* BADGER *lifts an eye, glances at him and goes
on with his paper.* MOLE *comes in. He looks at* TOAD.

MOLE Tut-tut! Again?

BADGER (*still reading his paper*) The third crash this
morning. There seems to be a good deal of traffic on
the road to-day.

MOLE Poor old Toad!

BADGER I always warned you, my dear Mole, that in
these cases the poison takes a long time to work itself
out of the system. But we're improving; we're improving daily. Let me see. It's Rat's turn to be on guard
this morning, isn't it?

MOLE Yes (*He helps* TOAD *up.*) Lean on me, old fellow.
That's right. Lie down a bit. (*He assists him towards a
camp-bed in the corner of the room.*) You'll be better

46

directly. I dare say Rat will read to you, if you ask him.

TOAD (*weakly*) Thank you, my dear friend, thank you. Don't let me be a burden to you.

MOLE That's all right, Toady. We'll soon get you well.

BADGER What do you say to a bit of a ramble along the hedgerows, Mole. And there's a new burrow I want to show you. I must say I like being out in this sort of weather.

MOLE (*eagerly*) Just what I was going to suggest. I wish old Ratty could come too. I suppose—

He looks across at TOAD.

BADGER No, no, it wouldn't be safe. (*In a whisper*) Toad's quiet now, and when he is quiet, then he's at his artfullest. I know him.

MOLE Yes, I suppose so. But it's such an exciting sort of day. Rat would love it so.

Enter RAT.

RAT Hallo, you fellows, not off yet?

BADGER Just going. (*He gets up.*) Toad's quiet now. But keep an eye on him. I don't trust him.

RAT That's all right.

MOLE (*quietly to* RAT) I believe he's worse than Badger thinks. Look after him well, poor old Toad.

RAT That's all right.

BADGER (*at the door*) Coming, Mole?

MOLE Coming. Poor old Ratty, it is a shame being kept in like this. Still we all have our turns.

RAT Of course we do. Good luck to you.

MOLE Good-bye!

BADGER Are you coming, Mole?

MOLE Coming! Good-bye! Good-bye, Toad!

TOAD (*faintly*) Good-bye, dear old Mole.

MOLE (*ecstatically*) What a morning! I don't think I ever remember—

BADGER (*severely*) When I was young, we *always* had mornings like this.

They go out. RAT, *after getting into an easier coat, turns his attention to* TOAD.

RAT Well, how are you to-day, old chap?

TOAD (*faintly*) Thank you so much, dear Ratty. It is good of you to inquire. But first tell me how you are yourself?

RAT Oh, *I'm* all right.

TOAD I'm glad! I'm glad! And the excellent Mole?

RAT Oh, *he's* all right.

TOAD Splendid, splendid! And the venerable Badger? He, I trust, is in robust health also?

RAT Rather! He and Mole have gone out for a ramble together. They won't be back till lunch.

TOAD Ah! (*Very faintly*) Dear fellows all!

RAT Now, old boy, we're going to have a jolly morning together, so jump up, and I'll do my best to amuse you.

TOAD Dear, kind Rat, how little you realize my condition, and how very far I am from jumping up now – if ever. But do not trouble about me. I hate being a burden to my friends, and I do not expect to be one much longer.

RAT Well, I hope not too. You've been a fine bother to us all *this* time, you have really, Toad. Weeks and weeks! And now, in weather like this, and the boating season just beginning! It's too bad of you!

TOAD I'm a nuisance to my friends, I know, I know.

RAT (*wistfully*) I was thinking about my river yesterday

ACT TWO · SCENE 3

evening, and I – I wrote a little poem. (*Shyly*) Do you think you would like to hear it?

TOAD   As you will, my dear Ratty. It may comfort my last hours.

RAT (*eagerly*)   It's about the ducks. I used to have such fun with them. You know when they stand on their heads suddenly, well, then I dive down and tickle their necks, and they come up all spluttering and angry, and shaking their feathers at me – of course they aren't angry really, because it's all fun – and then I used to sit on the bank in the sun, and pretend I was coming in after 'em again, and— (*He breaks off suddenly and announces*) 'Ducks' Ditty':

> All along the backwater,
>   Through the rushes tall,
> Ducks are a-dabbling,
>   Up tails all!
>
> Ducks' tails, drakes' tails,
>   Yellow feet aquiver,
> Yellow bills all out of sight
>   Busy in the river!
>
> Every one for what he likes!
>   We like to be
> Heads down, tails up,
>   Dabbling free!
>
> High in the blue above
>   Swifts whirl and call –
> We are down a-dabbling –
>   Up tails all!

> *He looks in front of him, seeing it all.*

TOAD (*with a deep sigh*) Thank you. I am glad to have
heard it. . . . Ratty?

RAT (*waking from his reverie*) Yes?

TOAD I wonder if I could bother you – but no, you
have been too kind already.

RAT Why, what is it? You know we'd do anything for
you, all of us.

TOAD Then could I beg you, for the last time probably,
to step round to the village as quickly as possible –
even now it may be too late – and fetch the doctor?

RAT (*surprised*) But—

TOAD No, you're right. It's only a trouble, and perhaps
we may as well let things take their course.

RAT But what do you want a doctor for?

TOAD Surely you have noticed— But no, why should
you? Noticing things is only a trouble. To-morrow,
indeed, you may be saying to yourself, 'Oh, if only I
had noticed sooner! If only I had *done* something! Too
late, too late!' . . . Forget that I asked. Naturally you
want to go on with your poetry. Have you ever done
anything in the way of epitaphs?

RAT (*alarmed*) Look here, old man, of course I'll fetch a
doctor to you, if you really want one. But it hasn't
come to that yet. You're imagining. Now let's talk
about something more cheerful.

TOAD (*with an angelic expression*) I fear, dear friend, that
talk can do little in a case like this – or doctors either,
for that matter. Still, one must grasp at the slightest
straw. And by the way – while you are in the village –
I hate to bother you, but I fancy that you pass the door
– *would* you mind asking my lawyer to step up? There
are moments – perhaps I should say there is *a* moment –
when one must face disagreeable tasks, at whatever cost

to exhausted nature. Thank you, my dear fellow, thank
you. You will not be forgotten.   *He closes his eyes.*

RAT   A lawyer! He *must* be bad. (*Aloud*) All right,
Toad, I'll go.

*He makes his preparations to go out, glancing from time
to time at the unconscious* TOAD *as he does so. Then a
brilliant idea occurs to him.*

RAT (*loudly*)   I'm going now, Toad.

TOAD (*faintly, his eyes closed*)   Thank you, thank you!

RAT   I'll bring the doctor and the lawyer, and we'll be
back as quickly as we can.

TOAD   You're a good fellow, Ratty.

RAT   Good-bye, old boy. Keep your spirits up.

TOAD   Good-bye!

Humming a tune and making a good deal of noise, RAT *goes
out. Then very quietly he steals back again and peers round
the door.* TOAD *is apparently still on the verge of dissolu-
tion.* RAT *nods to himself in satisfaction with his strategy;*
TOAD'S *illness is obviously genuine. We hear him as he
starts through the Wild Wood, singing 'Ducks' Ditty' to
himself. As the song dies in the distance,* TOAD *opens an
eye. Then the other eye. He raises his head and listens. He
sits up in bed, still listening. Then with a laugh he jumps
up and takes the floor.*

TOAD (*boastfully*)   Ha, ha, ha! Smart piece of work that!
(*He chatters to himself as he collects his coat, gloves, goggles,
money, and other accessories of outdoor life.*) Brain against
brute force – and brain came out on the top – as it's
bound to do. Poor old Ratty! My! Won't he catch it
when Badger gets back! A worthy fellow, Ratty, with
many good qualities, but very little intelligence – and
absolutely no education. I must take him in hand some
day, and see if I can make something of him.

He is ready now; as he goes to the door he begins to sing.
Really a most conceited song:

> The world has held great heroes,
>   As history-books have showed;
> But never a name to go down to fame
>   Compared with that of Toad!

He is singing the last line as he opens the door. Then with
a triumphant 'Poop-poop! Poop-poop!' he disappears.

Act Three

*

SCENE I · THE COURT-HOUSE

The Court-House. A bare, clean, white-washed room, furnished with a Bench, a Jury-Box, and a little extra space for the witness and spectators. It is crowded to-day, for the notorious TOAD *is to be tried, and there is every prospect that he will be sentenced to a severe term of penal servitude. In one corner, sitting gloomily together, are* BADGER, RAT, *and* MOLE. BADGER *has his handkerchief out. On the Bench the* JUDGE, *an owl-like gentleman, is sitting sipping a cup of tea. A figure, its head bowed in its hands, sits beside him. An* USHER, *tall and thin, wanders round the room with a list in his hand, ticking off those present. In the Jury-Box a* TURKEY, *a* DUCK, *four* SQUIRRELS, *five* RABBITS *and the* CHIEF WEASEL *are crowded together.*

USHER   One Judge. (*He looks at the Bench and marks off the* JUDGE *on his list.*) Twelve Jury. (*He counts them and marks them off.*) One policeman witness. (*To* POLICE-MAN) That's you. Now, don't you go a-moving or you'll muddle me. One policeman, and one prisoner. (*He looks at the Dock.*) Hallo! That's funny. Where is the prisoner?

POLICEMAN (*staggered*)   Well, I know I brought him in. (*Loudly*) Toad! Where are you?

TOAD (*looking up from the Bench, sadly*). Here I am.

USHER   What yer doing there? Come down out of it!

TOAD (*meekly*)   I thought this was where the prisoners went.

He glances at the JUDGE, *and comes down with a smirk.*

EVERYBODY   Did you hear what he said. . . . What was it? . . . Well, of all the cheek. . . . Just like Toad. . . . What was it? I didn't hear. . . .

And now, all being present, the USHER *walks up to the* JUDGE *and whispers in his ear. The* JUDGE *finishes his tea, and nods.*

USHER   Silence!

EVERYBODY (*to everybody else*)   Silence! Silence! Silence! . . .

JUDGE (*annoyed*)   Stop saying 'Silence!'

EVERYBODY (*to everybody else*)   Stop saying 'Silence'.

JUDGE   It's worse than ever! (*To* USHER) Try them with 'Hush'.

USHER (*in a loud whisper*)   Hush!   *Everybody hushes.*

JUDGE   Please understand, once and for all, that unless I have complete hush, it will be impossible for the prisoner to be tried.

TOAD   I don't want to be tried.

JUDGE (*sternly*)   Impossible for him to be tried, but not impossible for him to be severely sentenced.

BADGER (*in tears*)   Alack! Alack! Oh, hapless Toad!

TOAD   Well, it was fun anyway.

JUDGE (*clearing his throat*)   H'm! Friends and fellow-citizens! We see before us, cowering in the Dock, one of the most notorious and hardened malefactors of our time, the indigenous Toad.

TOAD   I'm not indigenous.

JUDGE (*grimly*)   Well, if you're not, you very soon will be. We see before us, I say, this monster of iniquity, and it is our duty to try him fairly and without prejudice, and to sentence him to the very sharpest term of imprisonment that we can think of, so as to learn him not to do it again. We shall then adjourn for lunch. (*Cries of 'Hear, hear!'*) It may be that after lunch we shall see things in a more rosy light, and be tempted to dilute justice with mercy, to the extent of remitting some thirty or forty years of the sentence. If so, we shall fight against the temptation. If, on the other hand, we see things in a more sombre light, and realize suddenly that we have been too lenient with the cowering criminal before us, we shall not hesitate to remedy our error. (*Kindly*) Has the prisoner anything to say before we pass on?

TOAD (*meekly*) No.

JUDGE Very well. Then I proceed to the charge. The counts against the prisoner are as follows. (*To* USHER) By the way, is the Jury all present? I particularly want the Jury to hear this. Just call 'em out and see.

USHER Certainly, m'lord. . . . Mr Turkey.

TURKEY Here!

USHER Mr Duck.

DUCK Here!

USHER Four squirrels!

SQUIRRELS Here!

USHER Six rabbits!

RABBITS Here!   RAT *rises and holds up his hand.*

RAT (*firmly*) I object.   *Sensation.*

JUDGE (*putting on his glasses*) What's the matter? Who is it? What did he— Ah, Ratty, my little friend, is it you? Delighted to see you. If you will just wait until I have got this ruffian off my hands, we can have a little talk. What about lunching with me? (*To* USHER) Go on, please.

USHER Six rabbits!

RABBITS Here!

RAT I object, my lord.

JUDGE (*surprised*) Object?

RAT One of the rabbits is a weasel.

CHIEF WEASEL (*indignantly*) I'm not! I'm a rabbit.

RAT He's a weasel.

JUDGE Dear, dear! A difference of opinion. (*To* USHER) What are we to do? What *does* one do?

USHER He *says* he's a rabbit, my lord, and he ought to know.

JUDGE (*to* RAT) There's something in that. You can't make a mistake about a thing of that sort.

RAT (*doggedly*) He's a weasel.

CHIEF WEASEL I'm not!

RAT That proves it. (*To* WEASEL) Why should you say you aren't, if you aren't?

JUDGE But of course he says he aren't if he aren't. I mean *if* he aren't, then he aren't, so naturally he says he aren't.　　　*He fans himself with his handkerchief.*

RAT But he wouldn't *say* he wasn't, if he wasn't. The other rabbits didn't say they wasn't. Why didn't they say they wasn't? Because they aren't.

JUDGE (*to* USHER) Just make a note that I shall want a glass of iced water if this goes on.

RAT (*eagerly*) Of course if you aren't, you don't say you aren't, but if you weren't, you would say you were.

JUDGE (*completely muddled*) But you wouldn't say you aren't, if you weren't, and on the other hand—(*Despairingly*) I think we'd better begin this trial *all* over again.

USHER Yes, my lord. Much the best way.

JUDGE (*to* RAT) You can tell me your objections after-

wards, when we have this desperate ruffian safely
lodged in a dungeon.

RAT He's a weasel! I know he's a weasel! You can see
he's a weasel! It isn't fair!

JUDGE (*soothingly*) There, there, there! We'll talk about
it calmly at lunch. There's a nice saddle of mutton –
and red-currant jelly.

MOLE (*boldly*) It's a shame, that's what it is, when
everybody knows what the weasels *are*.

CHIEF WEASEL (*to the* RABBITS) I'm a rabbit, aren't
I a rabbit? (*Under his breath*) Say I am— quick!

RABBITS (*terrified*) Y-yes.

CHIEF WEASEL There you are. Naturally there are
lots of different kinds of rabbit, and I'm one of the
different kinds.

RAT No, you're not.

CHIEF WEASEL Yes, I am.

JUDGE Please, please! For *my* sake. (*To* USHER) Now
then, *all* over again.

USHER (*stolidly*) Mr Turkey.

TURKEY Here!

USHER Mr Duck.

DUCK Here!

USHER Four squirrels.

SQUIRRELS Here!

USHER Five ordinary rabbits.

RABBITS Here!

USHER One different kind of rabbit.

CHIEF WEASEL Here!

USHER That's the lot, my lord.

ALFRED (*suddenly appearing*) What about me?

JUDGE (*putting on his glasses*) What *is* this?

ALFRED (in the USHER's *voice*) Alfred! (*Squeakily*) Here!

JUDGE (*to the* POLICEMAN) Lead it out.

ALFRED (*as he is led out*) All right, all right, I only just looked in. No *esprit de corps*. That's what's the matter with them all. No *esprit de corps*.

JUDGE Now then. (*Looking at his watch*) We haven't too much time. The counts against the prisoner are as follows: First, that he did maliciously steal a valuable motor-car without so much as a 'with your leave' or a 'by your leave'. Second, that being in the said motor-car, he did drive recklessly and to the common danger. Third, that on being apprehended he was guilty of gross impertinence to the rural police. (*Cheerfully*) Now then, Toad, what have you got to say about all that?

TOAD I wasn't driving recklessly. I was just going along quietly at about seventy miles an hour, when I saw a policeman in front of me. Naturally I quickened up to see if he wanted anything. Same as any one else would have done who's fond of policemen.

POLICEMAN Recklessly *and* to the common danger.

TOAD Rubbish!

POLICEMAN And what did you call me, eh?

TOAD How can I remember? Officer, constable, sergeant—

POLICEMAN No, you didn't.

JUDGE Now we're getting at it. What did he call you?

POLICEMAN (*annoyed*) He called me fat-face.

Sensation.

JUDGE (*aghast*) Fat-face!

EVERYBODY (*to everybody else*) He called him fat-face!

JUDGE This is terrible. This adds years to my life. (*To* POLICEMAN) You mean to tell me that this ruffian, this incorrigible rogue whom I am about to sentence to a severe term of penal servitude, had the audacity to call a representative of the Law 'fat-face'?

RAT   Oh, Toady!

BADGER   Alack! Alack! Oh, hapless animal!

JUDGE   Fat-face! Did I hear it aright? Fat-face?

POLICEMAN (*sulkily*)   We don't want to make a song about it. I told you what he called me, and that's what he called me.

USHER (*stolidly*)   Fat-face.

TOAD   I didn't mean *him* any more than any one else. I just murmured the expression to myself. It's a way I have. I'm that sort of person. I murmur things to myself. It's the result of a highly-strung temperament and an artistic nature.

USHER   He admits that he passed the expression 'fat-face', my lord, and that's good enough for any ordinary jury.

CHIEF WEASEL   Speaking as a special kind of rabbit, I say that it's good enough for *me*.

MOLE   Weasel!

CHIEF WEASEL   Shut up!

JUDGE   Very well. We have the prisoner condemned out of his own mouth of using most frightful cheek to a member of the rural police. We shall now sentence him severely.

USHER   Wait a bit, my lord. There's the little matter of stealing a valuable motor-car without so much as a 'with your leave' or a 'by your leave'.

JUDGE   Does it matter? I mean compared with this unspeakable impertinence to which the prisoner has already confessed?

USHER   Well, it adds more to the sentence, like.

JUDGE   Ah, well, in that case we must certainly go into

the matter. Well, Toad, what have you got to say about *that*?

TOAD I didn't mean to steal it. It was this way. I was just having a bit of lunch at an inn. I had been very ill – hadn't I, Ratty? – and my dear friends Mr Rat and Mr Mole and Mr Badger had been looking after me. It was the first time I'd been up and out, and I was having my bit of lunch – just a round of beef and a few pickled walnuts and a couple of helpings of treacle pudding – when I heard outside 'Poop-poop, poop-poop!'

JUDGE You heard *what*?

TOAD (*raptly*) Poop-poop, poop-poop!

USHER (*stolidly*) Imitation of motor-car.

JUDGE Oh! (*To himself*) Poop-poop! Poop-poop! (*Shaking his head*) No, I don't seem to get it.

TOAD Well, then two gentlemen came in to lunch, and as soon as I'd finished mine I went out to look at their car. I thought there couldn't be any harm in my only just *looking* at it. So I looked at it. And then naturally I began to say to myself, 'I wonder if this car *starts* easily.' So I wound it up just to see. And then naturally I stepped into the driver's seat, just as I always do, and – and then I saw a policeman with a very fat fa – with a very nice expression, a very *handsome* policeman, and he said, 'You're going a hundred and seventy miles an hour', and I said, 'Of course if you say so, dear Mr Policeman', and then—

JUDGE (*to* USHER) All this makes it worse, doesn't it?

USHER Much worse.

JUDGE (*relieved*) I thought so. It means we can give him a stiffer sentence?

USHER A much stiffer one.

JUDGE Good. You were saying, Toad?

BADGER (*rising weightily*) May *I* say a few words now, my lord?

JUDGE Who is this?

USHER Mr Badger, a well-known and highly respected member of the community.

JUDGE So it is, so it is. Well, Mr Badger?

BADGER Alack! Alack! O hapless Toad! O ill-fated animal.

JUDGE (*to* USHER) Is it a recitation?

BADGER I knew his father, I knew his grandfather, I knew his uncle, the Archdeacon.

JUDGE This makes it very serious indeed.

BADGER Many an afternoon have I spent in communion with his father at Toad Hall – one of the most attractive river-side residences with carriage-sweep.

JUDGE Dear, dear! *With* carriage-sweep, you say?

BADGER Unhappy day! O feckless Toad! O rash and ill-advised animal!   *He sits down again.*

JUDGE Most interesting. We are all indebted to Mr Badger for his profound and helpful observations. Now, I think, we can proceed to business.

CHIEF WEASEL Guilty!

JUDGE Of course he's guilty. That isn't the point. The only difficulty which presents itself in this otherwise very clear case is, how can we possibly make it sufficiently hot for the incorrigible rogue and hardened ruffian whom we see cowering in the Dock before us? Mr Usher, will you please tell us what is the very stiffest penalty we can impose for each of the three offences for which the prisoner stands convicted? Without, of course, giving him the benefit of the doubt, because there isn't any.

USHER Well, my lord, some people would consider

that stealing a valuable motor-car was the worst offence, and so it is. But cheeking the police carries the severest penalty, and so it ought. Suppose you were to say a year for the theft, which is mild, and three years for the furious driving, which is lenient, and fifteen years for the cheek, which is purely nominal; those figures, if added together correctly, tot up to nineteen years—

JUDGE First-rate!

USHER So you'd better make it a round twenty and be on the safe side.

TOAD (*meekly*) I don't mind if it isn't quite round.

JUDGE Silence! An excellent suggestion, Mr Usher. Now, prisoner, pull yourself together and try and stand up straight. It's going to be twenty years for you this time. And mind, if you appear before us again, on any charge whatever, we shall have to deal with you very seriously.

CHIEF WEASEL Hear, hear!

MOLE Shut up!

JUDGE Twenty years. Don't forget. Now then, prisoner, before the rest of us adjourn for lunch, is there anything you would like to say in the nature of a farewell speech? Any last words or valedictory utterances?

TOAD (*boldly*) Yes.

JUDGE (*kindly*) Well, well, what is it?

TOAD Fat-face!

JUDGE (*aghast*) Fat-face? ME?

TOAD (*wildly*) All of you! All the whole lot of you! All fat-faces! I am Toad, the Terror of the Highway; Toad, the Traffic-queller, the Lord of the Lone Trail, before whom all must give way or be smitten into nothingness and everlasting night. I am the Toad, the handsome, the popular, the successful Toad. And what are you? Just fat-faces.

JUDGE   Well, of all the ungrateful things to say!

TOAD   I am the great, the magnificent, the incomprehensible Toad!

RAT (*sadly*)   Oh, Toady, boasting again!

JUDGE   To call *me*, after all I've done for him, fat-face!

TOAD   The great Toad!   *He breaks into his chant:*

> The world has held great heroes,
>   As history-books have showed;
> But never a name to go down to fame
>   Compared with that of Toad!

JUDGE   Silence!

TOAD

> The clever men at Oxford
>   Know all there is to be knowed,
> But they none of them know one
>   half as much
>   As intelligent Mr Toad!

JUDGE   Stop him, somebody! Stop him!

TOAD

> The Army all saluted,
>   As they marched along the road;
> Was it the King? or Fat-face?
>   No. It was Mr Toad!

JUDGE   Take him away! Cast him into the dungeon! Load him with chains! Gag him!

EVERYBODY   Now then! Now then! Better come quietly!

TOAD (*as he is hustled away*):

> The Queen and her ladies-in-waiting
>   Sat in the window and sewed:

> She cried 'Look! who's that *handsome*
>   man?'
>   They answered, 'Mr Toad.'

*His voice is heard more and more faintly in the distance,
as he is led to the dungeons:*
Mr Toad! Mr Toad! Mr Toad!

A Dungeon. On a heap of straw in the corner, TOAD *sleeps uneasily. The door is unlocked, and* PHOEBE, *the jailer's daughter, comes in, with breakfast on a tray.* TOAD *sits up and takes the straw from his hair.*

PHOEBE Good morning, Toad.

TOAD (*gloomily*) Good morning, woman.

PHOEBE Slept well?

TOAD Slept well? How could I sleep well, immured in a dark and noisome dungeon like this?

PHOEBE Well, some do. . . . See, I've brought your breakfast.

TOAD Then you will oblige me by taking it away again.

PHOEBE What – aren't you ever going to eat any more?

TOAD You don't understand. This is the end.

PHOEBE You've said that every day for a month past. The end of what?

TOAD The end of everything. At least it is the end of the career of Toad, which is the same thing. (*He paces up and down.*) The popular and handsome Toad, the rich and hospitable Toad, the Toad so free and careless and debonair!

PHOEBE Cheer up, there's always hope.

TOAD Hope? How can I hope ever to be set at large again who have been imprisoned so justly for stealing so handsome a motor-car in such an audacious manner, and for such lurid and imaginative cheek bestowed upon such a fat, red-faced policeman?

PHOEBE Well, there *is* that, of course.

TOAD Stupid animal that I was, now I must languish in this dungeon till people who were proud to say they knew me have forgotten the very name of Toad.

PHOEBE There's no need to languish *all* the time.

TOAD (*with sobs*) Oh, wise old Badger! (*To* PHOEBE) A friend of mine. . . . Oh, clever, intelligent Rat and sensible Mole! – two other friends. What sound judgments, what a knowledge of men and matters you possess! Oh, unhappy and forsaken Toad!

PHOEBE (*arranging the breakfast*) Nice hot buttered toast and tea.

TOAD Oh, despairing and— Did you say *hot* buttered?

PHOEBE Made it myself, I did. Father said, 'Here's the key of Number 87,' he said, 'and you can take him his breakfast. He's the most notoriousest dangerous animal in the country,' said Father, 'and how we shall keep him under lock and key goodness only knows—'

TOAD (*brightening*). Did he say that?

PHOEBE His very words. 'The most notoriousest dangerous *and* reckless animal within the four walls of this here castle. And you can take him a couple of old crusts for his beakfast,' said Father, 'because I must starve and break his indomitable spirit,' said Father; 'otherwise he'll get the better of me.'

TOAD (*making a great effort to be modest*) Well, of course, one has one's reputation.

PHOEBE So I said, 'Yes, Father,' and as soon as his back was turned I said to myself, 'What a shame!' and I made this nice buttered toast.

TOAD (*his mouth full of it*) Believe me, girl, I am not ungrateful. You must pay me a visit at Toad Hall one of these days. Drop in to tea one afternoon.

PHOEBE Is that where you live?

TOAD (*nodding*) Finest house in these parts for miles around.

PHOEBE Tell me about it.

TOAD (*proudly*) Toad Hall is an eligible, self-contained gentleman's residence, very unique; dating in part from the fourteenth century, but replete with every modern convenience. Up-to-date sanitation. Five minutes from church, post-office and golf-links. Approached by long carriage-sweep.

PHOEBE Fancy! And do your friends Mr Badger and Mr Rat and Mr Mole live there with you?

TOAD (*laughing heartily*) Oh, my dear child! Badger! Rat! Mole! Excellent fellows all, but hardly – how shall I put it? – hardly (*with a wave of the paw*), well, hardly. They come to pay me a visit now and then, naturally; always glad to see them; but – well, quite frankly, they wouldn't be comfortable at a big house like Toad Hall, not to live. One has to be born to it. Badger lives in a rambling barn of a place near by; Rat has a little riverside villa; and Mole – well, really, I don't know where Mole does live. He's staying with Badger, I fancy, at present. Dear old Badger!

PHOEBE You're feeling better, aren't you?

TOAD The artistic temperament. We have our ups and downs.   *He returns to his breakfast.*

PHOEBE (*looking at him thoughtfully*) Now I wonder.

TOAD (*casually*) Any prisoners ever been known to escape from this castle of yours?

PHOEBE Never.

TOAD (*a little dashed*) Oh! ... Well, I must see what I can do. I must give my mind to it one day. Excellent buttered toast this.

PHOEBE *I've* been giving my mind to it lately.

TOAD That's the only way to make really good toast.

PHOEBE I didn't mean to that. I meant to escaping. I think I see a way in which you might do it.

TOAD (*dropping his toast in his excitement*) You're going to help me?

PHOEBE Yes. I like you, Toad, and I've felt sorry for you, and for your friends, who want to see you again so badly. And I think it's a shame the way you've been treated.

TOAD They were afraid of me, that's what it was.

He puffs out his cheeks.

PHOEBE Now listen. I have an aunt who is a washer-woman.

TOAD (*kindly*) There, there! Never mind. Think no more about it. I have several aunts who *ought* to be washerwomen.

PHOEBE Do be quiet a minute, Toad. You talk too much, that's your chief fault. Now my aunt does the washing for all the prisoners in the castle. Naturally we keep anything of that sort in the family. She brings the washing back Friday morning – that's to-day. Now you're very rich – at least you're always telling me so – and for a few pounds I think I could persuade her to lend you her dress and bonnet and so on, and you could escape as the castle washerwoman. You're very much alike in some ways – particularly about the figure.

TOAD (*indignantly*) We're *not*. I have a very elegant figure – for what I am.

PHOEBE So has my aunt – for what *she* is. But have it your own way, you horrid proud ungrateful animal, when I'm trying to help you!

TOAD (*quickly*) Yes, yes, that's all right, thank you very

much indeed. But I was only thinking— You surely wouldn't have Mr Toad, of Toad Hall, going about the country disguised as a washerwoman?

PHOEBE   All right, then you can stop here as a Toad. I suppose you want to go off in a coach and four?

TOAD   No, no! Please! You are a good, kind, clever girl, and I am indeed a proud and stupid Toad. Introduce me to your worthy aunt, if you will be so kind. It would be a privilege to meet her.

PHOEBE   That's better. (*As she goes out*) With a little trouble you'd make quite a nice Toad.

TOAD (*as the door closes*)   Chit!

He bursts happily into his song again, as he arranges a little collection of money – notes, gold, and silver – on the table, in such a way that it looks like an accident rather than a bribe. PHOEBE *returns with her* AUNT, *who appears to be dressed in a blanket. She has a bundle of clothes under her arm.*

PHOEBE   This is Mr Toad. My aunt.

AUNT   Good morning.

TOAD (*in his society manner*)   Good morning, dear lady. Charming weather we are having, are we not? Pray sit down. Your niece tells me that you – er – attend to the – er – that is, you have under your charge the habiliments, the more mutable habiliments of the inhabitants of the castle. A delightful profession, I am sure.

AUNT (*stolidly, to* PHOEBE)   Is this the one?

PHOEBE   Yes.

AUNT (*to* TOAD)   I wash.

TOAD   Quite so, quite so.

PHOEBE   I told you the idea, Aunt, didn't I?

AUNT (*eyeing the money*)   Some of it.

There is an awkward silence. PHOEBE *catches* TOAD'S
eye and indicates the money.

TOAD   Quite so. (*He clears his throat loudly.*) I was
wondering – naturally I shouldn't want to carry all my
money about with me – indeed, in the costume sug-
gested (*he indicates the bundle of clothes*) – I wondered if
you would oblige me so far – purely as a favour to
me—

AUNT   Is that the money?

TOAD (*indicating the money on the table*)   Just a little – er –
I haven't counted it—

AUNT   I have.

TOAD   Oh! . . . Well?

AUNT   Here you are.
*She hands over her bundle – cotton print gown, apron,
shawl, and rusty black bonnet.*

TOAD (*seizing the bundle*)   My dear lady, I am eternally
your debtor. Should you ever find yourself in the
neighbourhood of Toad Hall, a visit, whether professional or social— (*He holds up the dress.*) Er, how do
I—

PHOEBE (*much amused*)   I'll help you.

AUNT   You told him the condition?

TOAD   Condition?

PHOEBE   My aunt thinks she ought to be gagged and
bound, so as to look as if she had been overcome.
You'd like it, too. You wanted to leave the prison in
style.

TOAD (*beamingly*)   An excellent idea! So much more in
keeping with my character.

AUNT   I brought a bit of rope along, in case like.

TOAD   Splendid!

AUNT (*enjoying it*).   Got a nankerchief?

TOAD (*producing one*) Yes.

AUNT Then you gags me first. (*In a hoarse whisper*) Help! Help! Help! Help! Help!

TOAD (*carried away by the realism of this*) Silence, woman, else I gag thee!

AUNT (*undeterred*) Help! Help! Help!

TOAD (*advancing with gag*) Thou hast brought it on thyself. *He gags her.*

AUNT (*pulling down gag*) A little tighter, I think. . . . Help! Help! Help!

TOAD (*pulling it tighter*) A murrain on thy cackling tongue! There! (*To* PHOEBE) Now then, lend a hand with this rope.

PHOEBE How brave you are! *She lends a hand.*

TOAD (*regarding the* AUNT *with pride*) A neat bit of work that. Now then, how do I get into this?

He holds up the dress.

PHOEBE Silly, not like that. Here, give it to me. . . . Now then. (*She helps* TOAD *in, and does him up.*) Apron. . . . Shawl. . . . Now the bonnet. There! Well, upon my word, you're the very living image of her!

The AUNT *makes frantic indications of a desire to speak.*

TOAD What's the matter with her?

PHOEBE She wants to say something, I think.

She takes off the gag.

AUNT (*with conviction*) Too ugly.

PHOEBE Who is?

AUNT He is.

TOAD My good woman—

AUNT Much too ugly. Never do at all.

TOAD (*amazed*) Really—

AUNT Not a bit like me. Not good-looking enough.

TOAD Here, give me the gag!

AUNT Not *nearly* good-looking enough. Not—

> *But she is gagged again.*

PHOEBE Now then, Toad, we must hurry. I'll take you to the end of the corridor, and then you go straight down the stairs – you can't mistake the way – and if any of the jailers stop you and chaff you a bit – because she's very popular, Aunt is—

TOAD (*coldly*) I shouldn't have thought it.

PHOEBE Then you must give them a bit of chaff back, but respectable, of course, being a widow woman with a character to lose. Now good-bye and good luck.

TOAD (*nervously*) Good-bye, good-bye. If you're ever in the neighbourhood of Toad Hall—

PHOEBE Which I shan't be. Now, come on, there's a good Toad. You can thank me when you've escaped. Now, don't forget – you're a washerwoman.

> *She leads the way out.*

TOAD Yes, yes, we must be off. (*Nervously*) I wish I knew a little more what washerwomen talked about. (*In a falsetto voice, as he goes*) I remember once when I was ironing a shirt-front—

Early morning. A quiet spot by the canal bank. The tow-path cuts along by the edge of a wood, in which, just here, is a little clearing. At the entrance, half in, half out of a big hollow tree, lies a heap of old clothing; discarded, it would seem, by some washerwoman. . . . It moves. Evidently there is a washerwoman inside it. A voice comes from the interior. No, it is our friend TOAD.

TOAD (*sleepily*) I'll wear the light brown suit, and tell the car to be round at eleven o'clock. . . . No, leave the blinds down.   *He sleeps again.*
   Two baby rabbits come by with their MAMA, *on their way to school.*

FIRST BABY RABBIT (*Harold to the family*) What's 'at?
                                He gazes at TOAD.

MAMA RABBIT Now, now, come along, Harold, you'll be late for school.

SECOND BABY RABBIT (*Lucy*) What's Harold doing?

HAROLD (*rooted to the hollow tree*) What is it?

MAMA RABBIT Never mind now. Just some poor old washerwoman taking a rest. Come along, there's a good boy.

HAROLD May I play with it?

MAMA RABBIT After school, perhaps.

LUCY (*primly*) I like school. (*With an insufferable air of knowledge*) Twice two are four, twice three are six—

HAROLD May I play with it now?

MAMA RABBIT Not now, dear.

LUCY What's Harold saying?

HAROLD Do washerwomans know tables?

MAMA RABBIT I expect they do.

LUCY (*proudly*) I know my twice times. Twice two are four, twice three are six—

HAROLD What are washerwomans for?

MAMA RABBIT Now, now, come along. (*She takes his hand.*) Now, Lucy. (*She takes* LUCY's *hand.*) Now let's all run and see how quickly we can go.

> *They scamper off.*

HAROLD (*as they go*) Why do washerwomans—

> *But we hear no more.*

TOAD (*half waking again*) And tell Cook I'll have three eggs this morning, and be sure to give them each four minutes.... (*He moves and wriggles, and then slowly sits up.*) There, she's pulled the blinds up, and I told her— Hallo! (*He looks round him in amazement.*) Wherever— (*He stands up, looks at his clothes, looks round him again, and draws a deep breath of happiness.*) Aha! (*He chuckles.*) Toad again! Escaped from prison! Eluded his captors! Evaded his pursuers! The subtle and resourceful Toad!

> *He sits down in the sun, and idly removes a few dead leaves from his person.*
>
> *A* FOX *comes by, stops, and looks him up and down in a sarcastic sort of way.*

FOX Hallo, washerwoman! Half a pair of socks and a pillow-case short this week. Mind it doesn't occur again. *He goes off sniggering.*

TOAD Silly joke! Where's the humour of it? (*He stands up and spreads himself.*) If he had known! If he had only known who it was! Not a common washerwoman, but the great, the good, the entirely glorious Toad! (*He walks round and round in a circle, chanting his song*):

The world has held great heroes,
    As history-books have showed;
But never a name to go down to fame
    Compared with that of Toad.

The animals sat in the Ark and cried,
    Their tears in torrents flowed;
Who was it said, 'There's land ahead'?
    Encouraging Mr Toad!

The Queen and her ladies-in-waiting
    Sat in the window and sewed;
She cried, 'Look, who's that *handsome*
      man?'
    They answered, 'Mr Toad.'

(*In an ecstasy*) Oh, how clever I am! How clever, how very clever— (*He breaks off suddenly, as voices are heard crying, 'Toad! Toad! There he is! This way!'*) Oh, misery! Oh, despair!

    Terrified, he rushes into the hollow tree, and burrows under the leaves.

    The JUDGE, *the* POLICEMAN, *the* USHER, *and the* JAILER *come in.*

POLICEMAN   This way, your lordship. I heard him singing. All about himself. Just about here it sounded like.   *He begins to look round.*

JUDGE   Not that revolting song he sang when I had the pleasure of sentencing him to twenty years in a dungeon?

POLICEMAN   That's the song, your lordship. Only he had a new verse to it. Three verses he sang altogether.

JUDGE   As conceited as the old ones?

POLICEMAN Worse.

JUDGE Dear, dear. (*To* USHER) What's the penalty for singing conceited songs about yourself? Can I give him another five years?

POLICEMAN We've got to catch him first.

USHER Two years a verse is the usual.

JUDGE Good! Then that's six years. And say ten for having had the ingratitude to escape from a perfectly clean – (*to* JAILER) ventilated, you said?

JAILER Well-ventilated.

JUDGE Well-ventilated prison. That's another sixteen years. Excellent!

POLICEMAN We've got to catch him first. But he's about here somewhere, that I do say.

JAILER Just look in that hollow tree.

JUDGE He wouldn't be there, would he? Such a silly place to hide in.

POLICEMAN Well, you never know. (*He goes to it.* TOAD, *quaking in his fear, displaces the leaves.*) There's *something* there.

JUDGE Something undoubtedly.   *They all gather round.*

USHER A bird of some sort, most like.

TOAD (*brilliantly*) Chirp! Chirp! Chirp!

POLICEMAN Yes, you're right. Only a bird.

JUDGE Only a bird. What a pity.

USHER I knew it was only a bird. We're wasting time here.

JUDGE True. Lead on, policeman.

POLICEMAN Well, he's not far off. This way.

They all go off.

The leaves move again, and then TOAD'S *head peeps cautiously out.*

TOAD (*panting with fear*) Oh my! What an ass I am!

What a conceited and heedless ass! Swaggering again!
Shouting and singing songs again! Sitting about and
gassing again! Oh my! (*He stands up and looks round
cautiously. Then explores the clearing. The pursuit has died
away.*) Ah! That was good! Just a little resource, a little
cleverness! 'Only a bird.' Ha, ha, ha! That will amuse
the dear old Badger. I can hear his hearty laugh.
'We're wasting time here.' How the dear fellow, Mole,
will enjoy that! 'I knew it was only a bird.' The good
Rat will chuckle when I tell him.

> *He is standing with his back to the tow-path. A horse,
> dragging a tow-rope, comes along the path, stops, and puts
> his head ingratiatingly over* TOAD'S *shoulder.* TOAD'S
> *jaw drops. His knees tremble.*

TOAD (*terrified*) All right! I'll come quietly. (*He looks
nervously round, sees the horse, and gives a sob of relief.*)
You quite startled me! I thought it was— I said I'd
come quietly, just to put him off his guard. That was
all. Just to— Hallo! (*He sees the rope.*) A barge! Aha!
I will hail the owner and pitch him a yarn, and he will
give me a lift by a route which is not troubled by fat
policemen. Perhaps (*he heaves a sigh*) I may even get
some breakfast!

> *The horse has stopped and is cropping the grass. Evidently
> he is meant to stop here, for a comfortable-looking barge-
> woman comes in, carrying a bag of corn.*

BARGE-WOMAN A nice morning, ma'am.

TOAD The same to you, ma'am.

BARGE-WOMAN (*holding up bag*) Give the horse a bit of
breakfast.

TOAD (*with meaning*) The horse?

BARGE-WOMAN Had mine.

> *She ties the bag on to the horse's head.*

TOAD And a good hearty breakfast I'm sure it was, ma'am.

BARGE-WOMAN Well, I won't deny I like my vittals.

TOAD You're right, ma'am, you're right. (*Casually*) And finished it all up, I dare say – fried ham and eggs and – all of it.

BARGE-WOMAN (*with a laugh*) Pretty well, ma'am, pretty well.

TOAD Ah! (*He is gloomily silent.*)

BARGE-WOMAN (*having finished with the horse*) You seem in trouble, ma'am.

TOAD Trouble! Here's my married daughter she sends off to me to come at once. So off I comes, not knowing what may be happening, but fearing the worst, as you'll understand if you happen to be a mother too, ma'am. And I've left my business to look after itself – I'm in the washing and laundering line, as you can see, ma'am; and I've left my breakfast, I was that upset, and I've lost all my money and lost my way – and lost my breakfast, as you might say, too, and as for my married daughter – well, you know what it is, ma'am, being a married woman yourself, I dare say.

BARGE-WOMAN Dear, dear! Where might your married daughter be living?

TOAD Toad Hall, ma'am. The finest house in these parts, as no doubt you've heard tell. Tudor and Jacobean, my daughter tells me, with ornamental boathouse. That is, she lives just close to it.

BARGE-WOMAN Toad Hall? Why, I'm going that way myself. You come along in the barge with me, and I'll give you a lift.

TOAD I'm sure you're very kind, ma'am.

BARGE-WOMAN Don't mention it. So you're in the

washing business. And a fine business you've got too,
I dare say, if I'm not making too free in saying so.

TOAD Finest business in the whole country! All the
gentry come to me! Washing, ironing, clear starching,
making up gents' fine shirts for evening wear – all
done under my own eye.

BARGE-WOMAN But surely you don't *do* it all yourself,
ma'am?

TOAD Oh, I have girls, twenty or thirty of them always
at work. But you know what girls are, ma'am. Idle
trollops, that's what I call them.

BARGE-WOMAN They are that. And are you very fond
of washing?

TOAD I love it. I simply dote on it. Never so happy as
when I've got both arms in the wash-tub.

BARGE-WOMAN What a bit of luck meeting you!

TOAD (*nervously*) Why, what do you mean?

BARGE-WOMAN Well, look at *me*. I like washing too,
same as you. But there's my husband, who ought by
rights to be here now, steering or looking after the
horse, he has gone off with the dog to see if he can't
pick up a rabbit for dinner somewhere. Says he'll catch
us up at the next lock. Meantime, how am I to get on
with my washing?

TOAD Oh, never mind about the washing. Try and fix
your mind on that rabbit. Got any onions?

BARGE-WOMAN It's no good, I keep thinking of that
washing. And if it's a pleasure to you to do it, as you
say, being that fond of it, why then—

TOAD (*hastily*) No, no, I mustn't deprive you, not after
you've been looking forward to it for weeks, as I
expect you have. I'll steer, and then *you* can get on with
your washing in your own way. The fact is, I am more

used to gentlemen's things myself, shirt-fronts and cuffs – dressy things, if you know what I mean. It's my special line.

BARGE-WOMAN I dare say the other would come just as easy to you once you began. Besides, it takes some practice to steer a barge properly, when you've never done it before.

TOAD Never done it before? Why, ma'am, it's my own recreation – after wash hours. First thing I do, as soon as I can get away, is to go down to the canal for a bit of barge-steering. It's got hold of me, my friends say, almost like a disease. Fact is, it's always been in the family. My father owned twenty or thirty barges – big ones – never less than three horses pulling them – great big enormous ones—

BARGE-WOMAN (*with suspicion*) I don't believe you're a washerwoman at all.

TOAD (*indignantly*) Of course I'm a washerwoman! Should I be likely to say I was a washerwoman, if I wasn't? It isn't a thing you want to go about saying, if you aren't. Why should I be wearing a washerwoman's clothes if I'm not a washerwoman?

BARGE-WOMAN (*firmly*) Well, if you ask me, ma'am, I should say it's all a piece of deceit. I don't go for to say what you're doing it for, but what I do say is, that I won't have deceit on my barge. And that's for you, ma'am. *She goes to untie the bag from the horse's head.*

TOAD (*with dignity*) Oh, indeed, ma'am!

BARGE-WOMAN And I say this, ma'am, that if you have a daughter, which I dare say you haven't, I'm sorry for her, having a mother which practises deceit. (*She comes away with the bag.*) And I'll wish you good morning, ma'am. *She goes out, nose in air.*

TOAD (*shouting after her*) You common, low, fat barge-woman, don't you dare to talk to your betters like that. Washerwoman, indeed! I would have you know that I am the Toad, the Terror of the Countryside, the Scourge of Barge-women! Keep your stupid little barge! I prefer – riding! (*He unfastens the tow-rope, jumps on the horse's back and gallops off.*) The Toad! The Toad!

BARGE-WOMAN (*rushing after him*). Help! Help! The notorious Toad! Help!

> The POLICEMAN *and the others join in the pursuit.*

ALL   The Toad! The Toad!

Act Four
*

SCENE I · RAT'S HOUSE BY THE RIVER

Rat's river-side residence. In construction it is something like the cabin of a ship. Through the large port-holes at the back, the opposite bank of the river can be seen. . . . Rat is busy with a large heap of pistols, swords, and cudgels.

At one of the port-holes the head of the TOAD, *still wearing his washerwoman's bonnet over one eye, appears suddenly.*

TOAD (*from outside*) Help! Help!

RAT (*thoughtfully listening*) Funny! That sounded like Toad's voice.

TOAD Help!

RAT Yes, if Toad had been anywhere but where he is, poor unfortunate animal, I should have said—

He comes into TOAD'S *line of sight.*

TOAD Help! Help!

RAT (*turning round*) It is! Toady! However—

TOAD Give us a hand, Rat. I'm about done.

RAT (*excitedly*) Old Toad! (*He seizes hold of him.*) Well, this *is*— What's the matter? No strength left? *I* know. But however—?

TOAD You'll have to pull me in. I'm about done.

RAT That's all right. Got one kick left in you? Good!

Well, when I say, 'Kick', kick, and I'll pull, and— Now then, ready?

TOAD (*faintly*) Yes.

RAT Then – kick! (TOAD *kicks.* RAT *pulls, and he tumbles in on the floor.*) There!

TOAD (*gasping*) Oh! . . . Oh! . . . Oh!

RAT (*helping him up*). Come on the sofa a bit, won't you?

TOAD (*faintly*) Thank you, dear Ratty, thank you.

He flops on to the sofa.

RAT Here, drink this. You're about done.

He hands TOAD *a bottle.*

TOAD (*drinking*) Ah! (*He drinks again.*) That's better. I shall soon be all right. A passing faintness.

RAT (*looking at him*) Poor old Toady! And wet as wet. . . . And am I wrong, or *are* you disguised in parts as a washerwoman who has seen better days?

TOAD (*complacently*) Aha!

RAT That's more like you. Escaped, eh? In disguise?

TOAD (*more complacently*) Aha! (*He begins to sit up and take notice.*)

RAT That's much better. We'll soon have you all right.

TOAD It takes a good deal to put me out, Ratty. Just a passing faintness which might happen to any one who had been through what *I've* been through.

RAT You've been through a lot, I expect.

TOAD My dear Ratty, the times I've been through since I saw you last, you simply can't think!

RAT Yes. Well, when you've got those horrible things off, and cleaned yourself up a bit—

TOAD The times! Such trials, such sufferings, and all so nobly borne!

RAT You'll find some dry clothes upstairs—

TOAD Such escapes, such disguises, such subterfuges, and all so cleverly planned and carried out!

RAT Quite so. Well—

TOAD Been in prison – got out of it, of course! Stole a horse – rode away on it. Humbugged everybody – made 'em do exactly as I wanted. Oh, I *am* a smart Toad, and no mistake. Now what do you think my very last exploit was?

RAT (*severely*) I don't know, Toad. But seeing where it was I found you, and the state you were in, I should say that somebody had dropped you into the river, and then thrown mud at you. It isn't a thing to boast about, really it isn't, Toad.

TOAD Pooh, that was nothing. I just happened to be – to be heading a pursuit – on my horse – right in front of everybody else, in my usual way – and accidentally, not noticing the river in the enthusiasm of the chase – and the horse stopping a moment or two before I did—

RAT (*warningly*) Toad!

TOAD But I wasn't going to tell you about that. Now what do you think—

RAT (*taking him by the shoulders*) Toad!

TOAD Here, hold on a moment. I just want to tell you—

RAT Toad, will you go upstairs at once, and see if you can possibly make yourself look like a respectable animal again, for a more shabby, bedraggled, disreputable-looking object than you are now, I never set eyes on.

TOAD (*with dignity*) You can hardly realize, Ratty, to whom you are—

RAT Now stop swaggering and arguing and be off. Badger and Mole will be in directly—

TOAD (*airily*)   Oh, ah! Yes, of course, the Mole and the Badger. What's become of them, the dear fellows? I had forgotten all about them.

RAT (*gravely*)   Well may you ask!

TOAD   Why, what—

RAT   You will hear in good time. Badger himself may prefer to break the news to you. Be off now, and prepare yourself – why, what's the matter?

TOAD (*who has wandered in front of a mirror and is regarding himself with horror*).   Is this glass of yours all right?

RAT   Of course. Why?

TOAD   I hoped— You see, it's the first time I— You're quite right, Ratty. Nobody could carry off a costume like this. (*Meekly*) I'll go and change. (*He goes out.*)
  RAT, *left alone, fetches duster, pan, and brush, and begins to clean up after* TOAD, *murmuring 'Dear, dear!' to himself, and 'Well, I never!' While he is so engaged* BADGER *and* MOLE *come in.*

RAT (*eagerly*)   Hallo, here you are! I say, what do you think?

MOLE (*dropping into a chair*)   Too tired to think, Ratty, and that's a fact.

RAT   Yes, but—

BADGER (*gruffly*)   Nobody thinks nowadays. That's the trouble. Too much action, not enough thought.
                              He stretches himself on the sofa.

RAT   Yes, but—

MOLE (*to* RAT)   He's a bit low, just now. We've had a hard day. He'll be all right directly.

RAT   Yes, but what do you think? Toad's back.

MOLE (*jumping up*)   Toad! Back where?

RAT   Here!

MOLE   Where?

RAT (*with a jerk of the head*) Cleaning. You ought to have seen him, Mole. He'd have made you laugh.

BADGER (*with his eyes shut*) Unhappy animal!

MOLE Escaped?

RAT (*nodding*) 'M. So he says. But you know what Toad is.

BADGER I knew his father. Ah me!

MOLE Has he heard the news?

RAT Not yet. I said Badger would tell him.

MOLE Old Toad! ... He's just in time. Badger thinks it will be to-night!

RAT (*eagerly*) Not really?

MOLE Yes. *He* says so.

RAT I've been polishing up the pistols and cutlasses. They're all ready.

MOLE Good. We shall want all we can—

BADGER (*solemnly rousing himself*). Rat!

RAT (*turning round*). Hallo! ·

BADGER Did I hear you say that our young friend Toad has escaped from his noisome dungeon?

RAT Came in five minutes ago. In such a state.

BADGER I would speak with him.

RAT He's just having a wash.

BADGER (*severely*) This is no time for washing. We have work before us to-night. Hard fighting. Washing can wait. Where do you think *I* should have been if, at the crisis of my life, I had stopped to wash? Where would my revered father have been, if he had put soap before strategy? Where would my belovéd grand-father—

MOLE (*loudly*) Toady!

TOAD (*from outside*) Hallo, Mole, old fellow!

BADGER Thank you, Mole.   *He closes his eyes again.*

MOLE (*to* RAT)   I heard all about his belovéd grandfather this morning. Most interesting.

                              TOAD *comes in, almost his old self.*

TOAD (*cheerily*)   Hallo, you fellows!

MOLE (*delightedly*)   Toady!

BADGER (*solemnly rising*)   Welcome home, Toad! Alas! what am I saying? Home, indeed. This is a poor home-coming. Unhappy Toad!   *He sinks on to the sofa again.*

MOLE   Fancy having *you* back! And to-day of all days! To think that you have escaped from prison, you clever, intelligent Toad.

TOAD   Clever? Oh, no! I'm not clever, really. Badger doesn't think so. Rat doesn't think so. I've only broken out of the strongest prison in England, that's all. And disguised myself, and gone about the country on my horse humbugging everybody, that's all. Clever? Oh dear, no.

RAT   Oh, Toady!

TOAD   Well, I shall be strolling along to Toad Hall. One does get appreciated at home. Mole, if you like to drop in to coffee one evening, and care to hear a few of my milder adventures—

MOLE (*sadly*)   Oh, Toady, and you haven't heard!

TOAD   Heard what? Quick, don't spare me! What haven't I heard?

MOLE   The Stoats and the Weasels!

RAT   The Wild-Wooders!

MOLE   And how they've been and gone—

RAT   And taken Toad Hall—

MOLE   And been living there ever since—

RAT   Going on simply anyhow—

MOLE   Lying in bed half the day—

RAT   Breakfast at all hours—

MOLE Eating your grub and drinking your drink—

RAT And making bad jokes about you, and singing vulgar songs—

MOLE About—   *He hesitates.*

RAT About—   *He hesitates.*

MOLE Well, about prisons and magistrates, and police-men.

RAT Horrid personal songs with no humour in them.

MOLE That's what's happened, Toad. And it's no good pretending it hasn't.

RAT And they're all telling everybody that they've come to Toad Hall to stay for good.

TOAD Oh, have they! I'll jolly soon see about that!

RAT Yes, but how?

TOAD (*doubtfully*) Well – well – well, what I shall do—

RAT Of course, what you *ought* to do—

MOLE No, he oughtn't. Nothing of the sort. What he ought to do is, he ought to—

TOAD Well, I shan't do it, anyhow. I've been ordered about quite enough. It's my house we're talking about, and I know exactly what to do, and I'll tell you. I'm going to—

BADGER Be quiet, all of you! (*They are silent.*) Toad!

TOAD (*meekly*) Yes, Badger?

BADGER When you got into trouble a short time ago, and brought disgrace upon your own name, and shame and sorrow upon your friends, I resolved that on your return from your enforced seclusion, I would take the first opportunity of pointing out to you the folly of your ways.

TOAD (*meekly*) Yes, Badger. Thank you, Badger.

BADGER I even went so far as to jot down a few rough notes on the subject. Where are they, Rat?

RAT (*handing him a sheet of paper*) Here you are.

BADGER Thank you. (*Reading*) 'To make suet dump-
    lings—'

RAT It's the other side.

BADGER Ah yes, here we are.

TOAD (*meekly*) I'd rather have the bit about the
    dumplings, if it's all the same to you.

BADGER (*reading*) '(1) Conceit and its consequence. (2)
    Reverend Uncle, grief of. (3) Toad, whither tending?'
    (*He puts the paper down.*) But the moment for all this is
    past.

TOAD (*humbly*) Just as you like, Badger, old man.

BADGER The moment is past, because it is obvious
    now to everybody here where your folly has brought
    you. Toad Hall is in the hands of your enemies.
    Sentries guard it day and night. Unhappy Toad.

TOAD (*bursting into tears*) Alas, alas! Toad Hall, that
    desirable river-side residence, in the hands of Stoats
    and Weasels! This is, indeed, the end of everything!

                    He rolls on to the sofa in his grief.

BADGER Not quite the end. I haven't said my last
    word yet. Now I'm going to tell you a great secret.
    We are too few to attack from the front, but there is an
    underground passage that leads from the River Bank
    right up into the middle of Toad Hall.

TOAD (*sitting up brightly*) Oh, nonsense, Badger! I
    know every inch of Toad Hall inside and out. You've
    been listening to gossip, that's what you've been doing.

BADGER (*severely*) Right up into the middle of Toad
    Hall. When your father, who was a particular friend of
    mine, told me about it, he said, 'Don't tell my son.
    He means well,' he said, 'but he's very light and
    irresponsible in character,' he said, 'and simply cannot

hold his tongue. If he's ever in a real fix,' he said, 'and it would be of use to him,' he said, 'you may tell him. But not before.' That's what he said, Toad. Knowing the sort of animal you were.

TOAD Well, well, perhaps I am a bit of a talker. A popular fellow such as I am, my friends get round me, we chaff, we sparkle, we tell witty stories and somehow my tongue gets wagging. I have the gift of conversation. I have been told that I ought to have a *salon*, whatever that may be.

BADGER (*severely*) At present, my young friend, you haven't even got a box-room.

TOAD (*sweetly*) How true, dear Badger, and how well put. But you have a plan in that wise old head of yours. This passage. How shall we use it?

BADGER To-night the Chief Weasel is giving a banquet. It's his birthday. While they are all feasting, careless of the morrow, we four, armed to the teeth, will creep silently, by way of the passage, into the butler's pantry.

TOAD Ah! that squeaky board in the butler's pantry!

BADGER Armed to the teeth, you and Rat, by one door—

RAT (*looking up*) Yes, Badger.

BADGER And me and Mole by the other—

MOLE Yes, Badger.

BADGER Also armed to the teeth – we shall—

MOLE Creep out of the pantry—

RAT With our pistols, and swords, and sticks—

BADGER And rush in on them—

TOAD (*ecstatically*) And whack 'em and whack 'em and whack 'em.

BADGER Exactly. (*He pats* TOAD *on the back*). You have caught the spirit of it perfectly. Good Toad!

TOAD   I'll learn 'em to steal my house.

RAT   Teach 'em, Toad, not learn 'em.

BADGER   But we don't *want* to teach 'em. Toad's quite right. We want to *learn* 'em, and, what's more, we're going to. Now then, to rest, all of you. We start at 9 o'clock, and we must be fresh for it.

He settles down on the sofa.

RAT   I'll just get the lanterns trimmed.   *He goes out.*

MOLE (*settling down in a chair*)   Badger's right. I want a rest.

TOAD (*drawing a chair next to* MOLE)   Yes, we must rest. *He begins to chuckle.* MOLE, *eyes closed, takes no notice.* TOAD *glances at him and chuckles more loudly.* MOLE *lazily opens an eye.*

MOLE (*sleepily*)   Eh?

TOAD (*laughing heartily*)   I was just thinking – most amusing thing – really rather funny – I was in a hollow tree – and a policeman – well, a whole army of 'em, was looking for me – and one of 'em said, 'Is that a bird?' – ha, ha, ha! – really very funny – 'Is that a bird or what?' – and what do you think *I* did? – ha, ha, ha! – I said——   *And so on.* MOLE *sleeps.*

SCENE 2 · THE UNDERGROUND PASSAGE

The Secret Passage. The four conspirators steal in —
BADGER, RAT, MOLE, TOAD. BADGER *and* MOLE
carry the lanterns. They are all armed to the teeth.

BADGER (*to* RAT) H'sh!

RAT (*to* MOLE) H'sh!

MOLE (*to* TOAD) H'sh!

TOAD (*loudly*) *What?*

THE OTHERS H'sh!

TOAD Oh, all right.

BADGER We are now in the secret passage, but not
yet under the house. For the moment silence is not
absolutely necessary, but later on—

TOAD (*airily*) Quite so, quite so!

BADGER Now, it's all understood? Mole and I burst
into the banqueting hall by the east door, and drive
them towards the west door, where Rat and Toad—

TOAD (*impatiently*) That's all right, Badger. Let's get
at 'em.

BADGER Rat, you're responsible for the operations on
the western front. You understand? . . . What's the
matter?

RAT (*who is trying to read something by the light of* MOLE'S
lantern) Just before we start, hadn't we better make
sure we've got everything? (*Reading*) One belt, one
sword, one cutlass, one cudgel, one pair pistols, one
policeman's truncheon, one policeman's whistle—

TOAD *blows his loudly.*

BADGER (*alarmed*) What's that?

MOLE (*reproachfully*) Toad!

BADGER (*sternly*) Was that you, Toad?

TOAD (*meekly*) I just wanted to be sure it worked.

BADGER Now, Toad, I warn you solemnly, if I have any trouble from *you*, you'll be sent back, as sure as fate.

TOAD (*humbly*) Oh, Badger!

BADGER Well, I warn you.

RAT One policeman's whistle, two pairs of handcuffs, bandages, sticking-plaster, flask, sandwich-case. Now, has everybody got that?

BADGER (*with a laugh*) I've got it, but I'm going to do all I want to do with this here stick.

RAT It's just as you like, Badger. It's only that I don't want you to blame me afterwards and say that I'd forgotten anything.

BADGER Well, well! But no pistols, unless we have to. We shall only be shooting each other.

RAT Pistols in reserve, of course. Eh, Moly?

MOLE Of course. Eh, Toad?

TOAD (*who is examining his*) Of course.

It goes off with a tremendous bang. Everybody jumps.

MOLE (*reproachfully*) Toad!

BADGER Toad? You don't mean to say that that was Toad again? After what I've just said?

TOAD I – I just – I didn't—

BADGER Very well then, you go back.

TOAD (*falling on his knees*) Oh, please, Badger, please!

BADGER No! I can't take the risk.

TOAD Oh, Badger, please. After all I've been through – and my own house too. You *mustn't* send me back.

BADGER (*wavering*) I ought to.

MOLE Look here, I'll go last and keep an eye on him—

RAT   And we'll take his pistols and his whistle away. (*He does so.*)

BADGER   Well—

RAT   We'll leave 'em here, see. (*He puts them on the ground.*) Just here. It might be very useful, if we had to beat a retreat, to find a couple of freshly primed pistols and a policeman's whistle to fall back on. That'll be all right, Badger.

BADGER (*gruffly*)   Very well. (*He leads on.*) Now then, no more talking. From this moment absolute silence.

TOAD (*very humbly*)   Just before we begin the silence, Badger—

BADGER (*after waiting in silence*)   Well, what is it?

TOAD   A-a-a-a – tishoo! That's all. I felt it coming. Now I won't say another word.   *They pass on.*

The banqueting-room – a magnificent apartment – in Toad Hall. It being the CHIEF WEASEL'S *birthday, a banquet is in progress. The hero of the occasion, a laurel-wreath on his brow, sits at the head of the main table, his admirers round him. Pressed for a few more words, he rises.*

CHIEF WEASEL Friends and Fellow Animals. Before we part this evening I have one final toast to propose. (*Hear, hear!*) It is a toast which on all occasions has something of solemnity in it, something even of sadness, but never more so than on this occasion. 'Absent Friends.' (*Hear, hear!*) Absent Friends. With this toast I couple first the name of our kind host, Mr Toad. (*Loud laughter.*) Although unable to be present himself to-night – (*laughter*) – owing to a previous engagement – (*laughter*) – Mr Toad has generously put his entire establishment at our disposal for as long as we like to make use of it. (*Loud laughter.*) We all know Toad – (*hear, hear!*) – good Toad, wise Toad, modest Toad. (*Laughter.*) It is a personal sorrow to every one of us that he is not amongst us to-night. Let me sing you a little song which I have composed on this subject. (*Hear, hear!*)

> Toad he went a pleasuring
>   Gaily down the road –
> They put him in prison for twenty years:
>   Poor – old – Toad!

Toad he had a beautiful house,
   A most refined abode –
They put him in prison for twenty years:
   Poor – old – Toad!

Toad he had much money and goods
   All carefully bestowed –
They put him in prison for twenty years:
   Poor – old – Toad!

CHIEF WEASEL   Chorus, please.

   Poor – old – Toad!
   Poor – old – Toad!
   They put him in prison for twenty years:
   Poor – old – Toad!

Loud applause.

CHIEF WEASEL   But while we are thinking of our good host, Mr Toad, we must not forget our other absent friends – Mr Badger, Mr Rat and Mr Mole. (*Laughter.*) It is a particular sorrow to me that they are not with us to-night, living as they do – unlike Mr Toad – so very conveniently in the neighbourhood. From time to time, indeed, of late, we have caught glimpses of them – behind hedges. (*Laughter.*) We have seen their back views – (*laughter*) – in the distance – (*laughter*) – running away. (*Laughter.*) We know that they cannot plead absence from the country as an excuse for their absence from our board, so that the only reason for it must be excessive shyness. (*Laughter.*) Modesty. (*Laughter.*) All the more do we regret that they did not see fit to join us. Fellow animals, I give you the toast – 'Absent Friends!'
ALL (*rising and drinking*)   Absent Friends!

A DEEP VOICE OUTSIDE Absent Friends!

ALL (*to each other*) What's that? . . . What is it? . . . I didn't hear anything. . . . Nonsense. . . .

> *The door opens.* BADGER *and* MOLE *rush in.*

BADGER (*his war-cry*) Up the Badger!

MOLE (*his*) A Mole! A Mole!

BADGER (*wielding his cudgel*) Lay on to 'em, boys.

MOLE (*between blows*) Sorry we're late, Weasel – (*biff!*) – but many thanks all the same – (*biff!*) – for the kind invitation. (*Biff!*)

CHIEF WEASEL The other door! Quick!

> *The other door opens, and* TOAD *and* RAT *charge in.*

TOAD (*terribly*) I've come home, Weasel. (*He makes for him.*) How are *you*? (*Bang!*) Toad he went a-pleasuring, did he! (*Bang!*) I'll pleasure you! (*Bang!*)

THE ENEMY (*variously*) Help! . . . Mercy! . . . All *right*, all right! . . . I say, *shut* up!

BADGER Wallop 'em, boys. Keep walloping!

> *Some of the enemy are showing fight, some are escaping through the doors and windows, some are begging for mercy with uplifted paws.*

RAT (*to one of the weaker brethren*). Surrender, do you? All right. Get in that corner there.

> *There is a small rush for 'that corner there'.*

MOLE (*seeking whom he can devour*) A Mole! A Mole! (*To an unhappy Stoat.*) Hallo, were *you* looking for anything? (*Biff!*) Just wanted to say good-bye? (*Biff!*) *Good*-bye! (*Biff!*) Sorry you can't stop.

> *He biffs him out of the door.*

TOAD (*to a terrified Ferret*). Good evening! Do you sing at all?

FERRET N-no, sir, please, sir.

TOAD Not just a *little* song?

FERRET N-no, sir. I – I never l-learnt singing.

TOAD (*swinging his club*) Not just a *funny* little song about a poor old Toad?

FERRET (*with an effort*) N-no, sir.

TOAD (*ingratiatingly*) Try!

FERRET (*foolishly – in a high squeaky voice*) Poor – old – Toad!

TOAD (*furiously*) I'll learn you to sing!

> *With a squeal the Ferret scurries into* RAT'S *corner.*

RAT (*getting in front of* TOAD) All prisoners here, Toad. I'm looking after them.

> *He walks up and down in front of them, pistol in hand.*

BADGER (*walloping the last of the others out of the window*) There! That's the lot! (*He wipes his brow*). A pity! I was just beginning to enjoy it. What about your little party, Rat?

RAT They've surrendered. I thought they might come in useful, waiting on us and so on.

BADGER If any of 'em *wants* to go on for a bit longer—

CHORUS No, sir, please, sir.

BADGER Ah!

> *He looks round the room.* TOAD *is conducting an imaginary battle with a particularly stubborn adversary.*

TOAD (*getting his blow in*) Aha! (*Dodging an imaginary one*) That's no good. (*Getting another in*) More like *that*! . . .

BADGER Hallo! (TOAD, *recalled to himself, breaks off the engagement rather sheepishly.*) Now then, Toad, stir your stumps, and look lively. I want some grub, I do. We've got your house back for you, and you don't offer us so much as a sandwich.

RAT Just a moment, Badger. What about the sentries?

BADGER Sentries, yes.

RAT They may be still at their posts.

TOAD Sentries, pooh! They've run away far enough by now, haven't they, Mole?

MOLE If they're wise they have.

RAT I think it would be safer if Mole and I just—

BADGER Sensible Rat. There spoke the voice of wisdom. (*Picking up his cudgel*) You and I and Mole—

RAT Don't you bother, Badger. Mole and I—

BADGER (*grimly*) When I go walloping I *go* walloping.

TOAD So do I. Come on, I'll lead the way.

BADGER You will do nothing of the sort, Toad. You've asked us to stay to supper and we're staying to supper. Well, where is the supper? If this isn't your house, say so, and Mole can entertain us.

RAT (*indicating the prisoners*) They'll help you get it ready, Toady.

TOAD (*reluctantly*) Oh, all right.

MOLE (*to* TOAD, *as the others go out*) Don't forget the wine, Toad. We shall want to drink your health, and you'll have to make a speech.

TOAD (*cheering up*) Oh, right, right. That's all right, leave that to me.

> MOLE *goes out.* TOAD *is left with the now penitent prisoners – about eight of the smaller Stoats and Ferrets.*

TOAD (*to his slaves*) Now then, bustle up!

> *They bustle up eagerly.*

CHORUS Yes, sir, coming, sir!

TOAD Get busy.

CHORUS Yes, sir, please, sir!

TOAD I owe you a leathering apiece, as it is.

CHORUS Please, sir, no, sir!

TOAD Well, get busy, and perhaps I won't say any more about it.

> *They are very busy and the hall begins to look tidy again.*

TOAD (*sitting down at the head of the table*) Got a pencil, any of you?

ONE OF THEM Yes, sir.

TOAD (*taking it*) Thanks. . . . All right, don't hang about, get busy.

He takes a piece of paper from his pocket and begins to write.

THE PRISONERS (*whispering to each other*) He's writing. . . . He's writing a letter. . . . It isn't a letter. . . . It's *my* pencil he's using. . . . I wonder who he's writing to. . . . Shall we ask him what he's writing? . . . I will if you will. . . . *You* ask him, it's your pencil. . . . No, you . . . all right, I don't mind. . . . Well, go on then.

THE BRAVE ONE Please, sir—

TOAD (*proudly*) There!

THE BRAVE ONE Please, sir—

TOAD Now, I dare say all you young fellows are wondering what I've been doing?

CHORUS Please, sir, yes, sir.

TOAD Well, I've just been jotting down a few rough notes.

CHORUS Oo, sir.

TOAD Just a few notes for a little entertainment I have sketched out – a little informal singsong or conversazione to celebrate my return.

CHORUS Yes, sir, thank you, sir.

TOAD Something like this—

(1) Speech – By Toad.

And then I make a note. 'There will be other speeches by Toad during the evening.' Just so as to reassure people.

CHORUS Yes, sir.

TOAD (2) Address – By Toad.

Synopsis — you all know what that means, of course?

CHORUS Please, sir, no, sir.

TOAD Well, it just means – well, you'll see what it means directly. It's just a sort of synopsis.

CHORUS Yes, sir.

TOAD Synopsis. Our Prison System – The Art of Disguise – Barge Life – Steeple-chasing and its dangers – A Typical English Squire.

CHORUS Yes, sir.

TOAD (3) Imitations of Various Bird Notes. By Toad.
(4) Song – By Toad. (Composed by Himself.)
(5) Other compositions by Toad. (Sung by the Composer.)
(6) Song. 'For He's a Jolly Good Fellow.' (Sung by Badger, Rat, and Mole.)

CHORUS Oo, sir.

TOAD That's all, just a few rough notes. Of course it may shape a little differently as the evening goes on. There are one or two conjuring tricks which I used to know – something to do with three billiard balls and a globe of goldfish – they may come back to me or they may not. We shall see.

CHORUS Yes, sir, thank you, sir.

THE BRAVE ONE Could you give us the song now sir?

TOAD (*pleased*) Give it you now, eh?

CHORUS Oo, please, sir.

TOAD Well, well.

> *He gets up and walks to the middle of the room.*

THE BRAVE ONE (*picking up the* CHIEF WEASEL'S *wreath*) Wouldn't you like to wear this, sir?

TOAD You think – eh?— Well, perhaps you're right.

> *He puts it on.*

CHORUS Oo, *sir*!

TOAD Suits me, eh?

CHORUS Please, sir, yes, sir.

TOAD Some people can wear 'em and some can't. You have the manner or you haven't. There it is. You can't explain it.

CHORUS Yes, sir. Where will you stand, sir?

THE BRAVE ONE (*bringing a stool*) Won't you stand on this, sir?

TOAD (*modestly mounting*) Well, perhaps—

CHORUS Oo, *sir*!

TOAD Now this is just a *little* song, and it's called 'When the Toad came Home.'

CHORUS Yes, sir.

TOAD There's only one verse at present, but it can be sung any number of times.

THE BRAVE ONE Yes, sir. May we all sing it?

TOAD Certainly, certainly. It is really composed with the idea of being sung by a great many people.

CHORUS Yes, sir.

> *They group themselves round him, expectantly.*

TOAD (*solemnly*) 'When the Toad came Home.'

> *Singing.*

The Toad – came – home!

There was panic in the parlour, there was howling in the hall,

There was crying in the cow-shed and a snorting in the stall,

There was smashing in of window, there was crashing in of door,

There was bashing of the enemy who fainted on the floor,

When the Toad – came – home!

> *All the prisoners dance in a circle round* TOAD, *singing*

this song. TOAD *stands wreathed above them, raptly enjoying it. In the middle of the second verse* BADGER, RAT *and* MOLE *return.*

BADGER (*appalled*)   Toad! Get down at once!

TOAD *does not hear him. He is far away. The singers finish their verse, but go on dancing round the hero.*

MOLE (*reproachfully*)   Toad!

RAT (*to* BADGER)   It's no good. I know him. He's practically in a trance. Let him have his evening out.

MOLE   We'll talk to him in the morning.

RAT   Talking's no good to Toad. He'll always come back to what he is.

BADGER (*grimly*)   All the same, I'll talk to him.

RAT   But let him have his hour first.

BADGER   Oh, all right.

They stand watching. The dancers are singing again now. . . .

MOLE (*apologetically*)   You know, there's something about that tune. . . . It's only just . . . I shan't be . . .

And suddenly he is in the circle, dancing and singing.

BADGER   He's very young still, is Mole.

RAT   Y-yes.

BADGER   The best of fellows, of course. But young, young.

RAT   Y-yes. . . . All the same, I don't see why . . . I mean, after all . . . I . . . well, I . . . Excuse me!

And now he, too, is in the circle.

But others seem to have heard the news. The Jury come on, singing and dancing—

JURY

There were calls from all the neighbours,
    there were letters from afar –

– followed by the JUDGE *and the* USHER.

JUDGE

There was groaning on the Bench –

USHER

– and there was moaning at the Bar.

Then PHOEBE –

PHOEBE

There was tooting on the piccolo and fluting on the
pipes.

– and the WASHERWOMAN *and* BARGE-WOMAN.

WOMEN

There was starching of 'is sockses and a washing of
'is wipes,

ALL

When the Toad came home, When the Toad came
home.

Enter ALFRED

ALFRED

There was shrieking in the gear-box, there was
trumpeting of horn,

And the elephant was jealous and the parrot felt
forlorn.

ALL

There were speeches from the gentry, there was
moistening of throats,

Enter POLICEMAN

POLICEMAN

And a moistening of pencils and a taking down of
notes.

ALL

When the Toad came home, When the Toad came
home.

Now they are all round TOAD, *singing and dancing; all
but* BADGER.

BADGER Well, well, well! (*Doubtfully*) Well— (*Less doubtfully*) W-w-well? (*His mind made up*) Oh, well!
He joins the dancers, and hobbles stiffly round with them.

ALL
There was welcoming to Badger, when he joined the merry throng.

BADGER
I can do it for a little but I can't go on for long. . . .
And so on. The incense of their adoration streams up to the be-laurelled TOAD, *and with a long sigh of happiness he closes his eyes.*

Epilogue

*

THE WIND IN THE WILLOWS

It is Spring again. The wind is whispering in the willows that fringe the river. Faintly we hear its elfin music. Among her daffodils lies MARIGOLD, *in tumbled sleep. The dead leaves in the hollow rise and fall; they fall apart as an old grey* BADGER *heaves himself into the sunlight. Curiously he sniffs at* MARIGOLD, *and then lumbers away. A* WATER-RAT *twinkles out of his hole in the bank; a* MOLE *laboriously takes the air; they, too, pass the time of day with* MARIGOLD *before following in the wake of the* BADGER. *Last of all comes a* TOAD. *'Ah Marigold, Marigold!' – and so, waddling jauntily, after the others. . . .*
But NURSE *is getting impatient. From afar her voice comes to us.*

NURSE   Marigold! Marigold! It's time we went, dear!
MARIGOLD *sighs gently, and stirs a little in her sleep.*